INSIGHT POCKET GUIDE

Seville
Córdoba & Granada

APA PUBLICATIONS

Part of the Langenscheidt Publishing Group

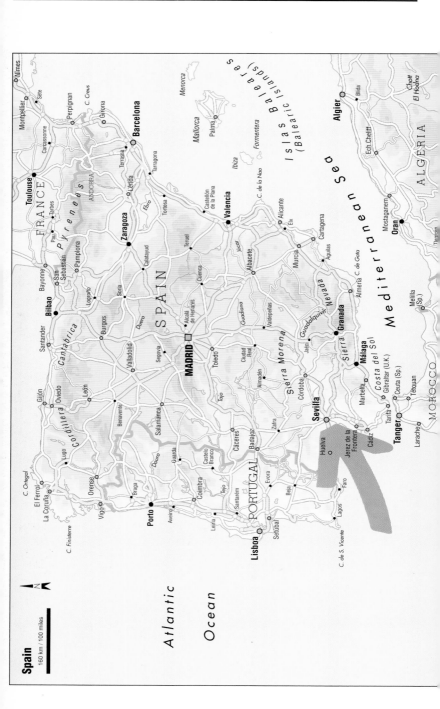

introduction

Welcome

This guidebook combines the interests and enthusiasms of two of the world's best-known information providers: Insight Guides, who have set the standard for visual travel guides since 1970, and Discovery Channel, the world's premier source of non-fiction television programming. Its aim is to help visitors get the most out of a short stay in Southern Spain's three great cities, Seville, Córdoba and Granada by using a series of itineraries designed by Nigel Tisdall, Insight Guides' specialist on the region. The tours cover all the must-see highlights – Seville's Cathedral and Giralda tower, Córdoba's Mezquita and Granada's Alhambra – but they also explore the old Jewish and Moorish quarters beyond the blockbuster sights, with frequent recommendations for shopping, lunch and *tapas* en route. In addition to the city tours there are three excursions into the countryside around the cities, to the Doñana National Park from Seville; to the Montilla and the Sierra Subbética from Córdoba; and into the Sierra Nevada and the Alpujarra from Granada. Supporting the itineraries are sections on history and culture, eating out, shopping and practical information, including a list of recommended hotels.

Nigel Tisdall first visited Andalusia in the mid-1980s, travelling there by train, in an old stiff-backed compartment decorated with lace curtains and table lamps. While researching this guide, he again took the train, but this time a Talgo, a sleek express complete with video screens. He describes Andalusia as one of the most exhilarating regions of Spain. 'It will always be a hotbed of Spanish cliché – the birthplace of flamenco, the cradle of bull-fighting, a playground for gypsy passion, but it is brimming with energy, and Seville has become one of the most fashionable, hi-tech cities in southern Europe.'

This edition of the guide was updated and expanded by **Mark Little**, a regular contributor to Insight Guides, who lives on the Costa del Sol.

10 City Walks and Museums explores the eastern part of the city, including the fine arts museum and the Palacio de los Marqueses de Viana. It ends with a visit to Medina Zahara, 8km (5 miles) from Córdoba **47**

11 Montilla and the Sierra Subbética is an excursion into the countryside south of Córdoba **50**

GRANADA

12 Alhambra: Alcazaba and Generalife concentrates on the ancient fortress and the Nasrid rulers' summer residence **53**

13 Alhambra: Nasrid Palaces and Gardens explores the most captivating part of the Alhambra, including the Court of the Myrtles, the Hall of the Ambassadors, the Court of the Lions and the Baño de Comares.............. **57**

14 Exploring the Albaicín focuses on the pretty streets of the steep hill facing the Alhambra........................... **60**

15 The Cathedral Quarter focuses on an area often neglected by visitors. As well as the cathedral, it takes in La Madraza **62**

16 Sierra Nevada and the Alpujarras explores the glorious region around Granada **64**

LEISURE ACTIVITIES

Best buys, best restaurants, best nightlife and a guide to sports opportunities... **67–77**

CALENDAR OF EVENTS

A guide to festivals in the three cities................... **78–79**

PRACTICAL INFORMATION

All the background information you are likely to need for your stay, with a list of hand-picked hotels........... **81–91**

MAPS

Spain 4
Andalusia 18–19
Seville 22
Seville Cathedral.......... 25
Real Alcazares 26
Córdoba 43
La Mezquita 45
Granada 55
Alhambra I 56
Alhambra II 59

CREDITS AND INDEX

pages **93–96**

Pages 2–3: the Alhambra
Pages 8–9 Seville's Plaza de España

History & Culture

The history of the Río Guadalquivir, one of Spain's great rivers, reflects that of the south of the country. Now bloated with silt, it is a portly descendant of the fast-flowing, frequently flooding Baetis (Blessed) river that the Romans knew. From the mountains of northeastern Jaén, its waters wend their way westwards for some 600km (375 miles), carving an ever-widening valley that culminates in Las Marismas. These broad marsh-lands stall its entry into the Atlantic beside the sherry town of Sanlúcar de Barrameda. When their fleets arrived here in the 1st century BC the Romans could sail upriver as far as Córdoba, a strategic point already colonised by Phoenician, Carthaginian and Iberian settlers.

Birthplace of Trajan and Hadrian

The Romans laid the ground plan of southern Spain, building roads, bridges and aqueducts. They established Córdoba, the home of Seneca and Lucan, as the capital of Hispania Ulterior, and redeveloped many of the prehistoric settlements built alongside the Baetis, including Hispalis (now Seville), Carmona and Itálica. The vicinity's numerous archaeological excavations have produced many an artefact that now graces the museums and stately homes of Seville and Córdoba. Of these the most famous is the gold jewellery that constitutes the Carambolo treasure in Seville's Museo Arqueológico. This incredible collection testifies to the wealth of the kingdom of Tartessus that flourished here in the 8th and 9th centuries BC. Near Santiponce (on what are now the western outskirts of Seville) you can wander amid the crumbling ruins of Roman Itálica, birthplace of the emperors Trajan and Hadrian, while at Carmona you can see the remains of the necropolis and amphitheatre.

The fall of the Roman Empire led to the rise of the Visigoths, who set up their capital in Toledo. A number of Visigoth fountains, arches and columns can still be seen lurking inside Andalusian monuments constructed many centuries later. In AD711 the Moors – principally Arabs and North African Berbers – landed at Tarifa. This arrival marked the start of a phenomenal advance: in seven years the Moors conquered virtually the whole peninsula. What had begun as a daring foray was to result in eight centuries of Moorish rule and the flowering of a great civilisation.

The Moors called their new land al-Andalus, and the river that fed it Guad-al-Quivir (Great River). By the 10th century, Córdoba, the capital of al-Andalus, had become the most important city in Europe. It was four times its present size, and had a university, libraries, public baths, work-shops, street-lighting and more than 1,000 mosques.

Left: the richly decorated dome of Córdoba's La Mezquita
Right: a Tartessian mask dating back to the 8th or 9th century BC

The greatest of these, La Mezquita, still stands as a testimony to this golden age, which reached its apogee with the construction of the palaces at Medinat al-Zahra (now Medina Zahara, just outside Córdoba). Today their partly restored ruins barely hint at the opulence of a royal pleasure park that had its own zoo, mint, fabric factory and arsenal. At its centre stood a pool filled with mercury; when stirred, the sunlight's reflection would flash round the surrounding marble patios and the gold and silver tiles of the roofs.

Moors Bearing Gifts
Fabulous wealth grew from the Moors' talent for irrigation in the rich lands of the Guadalquivir Valley. The Greeks had introduced the vine and the olive – both cultivated intensively by the Romans – but it was the Arabs who added the orange and the almond tree, along with rice, aubergines, saffron, cotton, silk-farming, Merino sheep and herbs, spices and fruits. They also, like the Phoenicians before them and the British long after, exploited the mineral resources of the surrounding sierras.

Inevitably, it did not last. By the 11th century the refined glory of the Umayyad Caliphate had disintegrated into feuding *taifas* (factional kingdoms). These were easily overrun by the strict and austere Almoravids,

The Ubiquitous Christopher Columbus

In 1485 the Genoan-born Christopher Columbus (1451–1506) travelled to Iberia to elicit support for his 'Enterprise of the Indies' – a voyage intended to reach the shores of the East by sailing west across the Atlantic. Aged 34, Columbus (who may have been of Spanish-Jewish descent) a widower with a five-year-old son, had prematurely white hair, and had already sailed to Madeira, Iceland and the Gold Coast.

After a rejection by the Portuguese court, he sought an audience with Ferdinand and Isabella. The commission they ordered to assess his proposals took four years to reach its verdict: 'vain and worthy of all rejection'. Columbus retreated to the monastery of La Rábida, near Huelva, but its prior, who had been Isabella's confessor, managed to get him recalled to the court.

Columbus sailed on 3 August 1492 from Palos de la Frontera (near Huelva) with three caravels, *Nina*, *Pinta* and *Santa María*. On 12 October they sighted land – a Bahama island – and a few hours later the Spanish flag was planted in the New World.

The great mariner made three further voyages. In 1493 he sailed from Cádiz and dis-covered Puerto Rico and Jamaica; in 1498 he sailed from Sanlúcar de Barrameda and reached the mouth of the Orinoco; in 1502, sailing from Seville, he discovered Panama. In the last years of his life he went to live in Santa María de las Cueva, a Carthusian monastery west of Seville, where he wrote four autobiographical books, mourned the loss of his governorship over lands he discovered, and hatched new plans, such as the liberation of Jerusalem. The restored monastery was the centrepoint of Expo '92 and is now a museum.

After Columbus died in Valladolid in 1506, his remains undertook a mysterious voyage of their own. In 1509 they were brought back to La Cartuja, but were exhumed again in 1536 – perhaps being transferred to Seville's cathedral. Around 1544 they were shipped to the Caribbean island of Santo Domingo (the Dominican Republic), but were later moved to Havana cathedral; they were returned to Seville cathedral in 1899. What ended up where is anybody's guess, but one thing is certain: an awful lot of places can stand up and say with all honesty 'Columbus was here'.

whose Berber armies were summoned to prevent a Christian reconquest. They in turn were succeeded by the more liberal Almohads, who established their capital in Seville – the greatest of the *taifas* – and bequeathed us the Giralda and Torre del Oro as mementoes of their reign.

The Decline of al-Andalus

In 1212 the Christians defeated the Almohads at Las Navas de Tolosa in the Sierra Morena, a turning point in the 700-year *Reconquista*. By 1236, Ferdinand III had captured Córdoba, and in 1248 he took Seville. Ferdinand was aided by the complicity of the first Nasrid king, Ibn-al-Ahmar, who had retreated from Jaén to the mountains of the Sierra Nevada and a new power base in the former Almoravid capital of Granada. As a result of a peace treaty with the Christians, the kingdom of Granada – which covered the modern provinces of Málaga, Granada and Almería – survived as a vassal state for 250 years. The city flourished, not least due to an influx of Muslim refugees and artisans from other captured cities. Indeed the new-comers played a key role in building the Alhambra, the Nasrid dynasty's memorial to the swansong days of al-Andalus. At the same time the Christian king Pedro the Cruel was also employing Moorish craftsmen to build another tribute to this fading world – the Alcázar in Seville.

In 1492 the Catholic monarchs Ferdinand and Isabella captured Granada, Columbus discovered the New World, and the Jews were expelled from Spain. By then the notorious Inquisition had been in force for 12 years (it was to survive until 1821), *autos-da-fé* (burnings of heretics) were a fact of Sevillian life, and *conversos* (converted Jews) were having their wealth confiscated for investment in projects such as Columbus's second voyage. In 1503 the monopoly of trade with the New World was awarded to Seville's Casa de la Contratación, from which the city reaped

Above: life in Moorish Spain
Right: the Moors admit defeat

great profits. One of its employees, Amerigo Vespucci, gave his name to the new continent, Hernando Cortés sailed from Seville to ravage Mexico, and Ferdinand Magellan circumnavigated the globe. *Conquistadores* returned laden with gold and new curiosities such as peppers, tomatoes, quinine and tobacco.

By 1588 Seville had a population of at least 80,000, and a stature equal to that of Venice. But from the end of the 16th century it embarked on a slow, glorious descent into decadence, a decline exacerbated by the expulsion of the *moriscos* (converted Moors) in 1610 and a terrible plague in 1649. During the 16th and 17th centuries Seville acted as a transit point for trade, administration and emigration. Its Lonja (Exchange), financed by a quarter-percent tax on the import of silver, is now the Archive of the Indies, where you can see the signatures of these early colonisers.

Church Wealth

These were heady days in Seville. Miguel de Cervantes (1547–1616), who served time in Seville's prison, recorded its colourful, roguish underworld in his novels; Bartolomé Esteban Murillo (1617–82) painted the beggars and other characters that filled the city's crowded streets. The Church, its coffers filled to bursting by the activities of the Inquisition, acquired a wealth that enabled it to build for itself luxury city-centre sanctuaries that to this day force pedestrians into circumnavigatory detours. At one point the city had

Architectural Terms

Alcázar: Moorish palace
Alcazaba: Moorish castle
Aljibe: cistern
Artesonado: inlaid, coffered wooden ceiling, often with star-shaped patterns
Azulejo: coloured and patterned glazed ceramic tile
Mudéjar: work carried out by Moorish craftsmen under Christian rule
Mozarabic: work by Christian crafts-men under Moorish rule
Patio: inner courtyard
Plateresque: A Renaissance style characterised by richly ornamented surface decoration, similar to that wrought by a *platero* (silversmith).

more than 70 convents, a glut mitigated only by their decorations, which often featured paintings and sculpture by artists such as Velázquez, Cano, Zurbarán, Murillo and Leal – all members of what is now referred to as the Seville School. Their works can be seen in Seville's excellent Fine Arts Museum.

In 1717 the silting of the Guadalquivir forced the Casa de la Contratación to be moved south to Cádiz, thus hastening official recognition of Seville's decline. Córdoba and Granada were now merely provincial backwaters in a demoralised country whose empire had been shrivelled by the 1701–14 War of the Spanish Succession. In the 18th and 19th centuries Andalusia gained a reputation as the home of gypsies, brigands, *majos* (dandies) and matadors that enchanted northern Europeans. Seville was seen as a city of aristocratic seducers called Don Juan and street-wise barbers called Figaro, while a sultry gypsy girl by the name of Carmen worked in the heat of its famous tobacco factory. In reality, however, Andalusia was a place of political chaos and deep poverty: by the beginning of the 19th century, 72 percent of the farming land in Seville was owned by an elite and invariably absentee land-lord class that comprised barely five percent of its population.

Travellers and Romantics

Poverty contributed to the appeal of southern Spain for the numerous aristocratic travellers who hired mules, boats and carriages to tour its provinces. They enjoyed its dilapidated state, exotic landscape and Moorish-Oriental heritage. The Alhambra – now a picturesque ruin – inspired many a Romantic eulogy. Washington Irving swam in its ancient pools, Théophile Gautier cooled sherry in its fountains and hotels appeared on the hill. But it was the passionate, sensual lifestyle of the Andalusians that really set northern hearts pumping. Hans Christian Andersen, visiting Andalusia in the 1860s, admitted his disappointment that he had experienced 'just a little encounter with bandits'. One intrepid lady traveller, en route to the Sahara in the same period, confessed that, after hearing a guitarist in Granada, 'you are ready to make love and war'.

Spain – which meant Andalusia to these visitors – was in vogue. This fashion was encouraged by the nation's victories in the Peninsular War (1809–14), its low cost of living and the growth of trade interests such as sherry. Granada and Seville topped the bill of places to see: 'Seville, the marvel of Andalusia, can be seen in a week' declared Richard Ford in his 1845 *Handbook for Spain*, a masterly work that did much to put Spain on the tourist map. Córdoba tended to receive, as it does today, a more perfunctory inspection.

By the end of the 19th century, Spain had lost virtually all of its remaining colonies, and it still lacked political stability. The nation remained neutral in World War I but in the 1920s it became bogged down in a war of independence with its one-time masters, the Berber tribes of Morocco. In an attempt to create a lasting order out of chaos, General Miguel Primo de Rivera assumed power in a semi-dictatorship that had the

Above Left: bust of Cano, an artist of the Seville School
Right: the legendary Carmen

concurrence of King Alfonso XIII: the pastiche pavilions built for the 1929 Ibero-American Exposition in Seville are a legacy of his period of power.

In the 1930s Ernest Hemingway wrote *Death in the Afternoon*, a paean to the 'noble art' of bullfighting, but it was fighting of a different nature that characterised that decade in Spain. Almost one million people were killed in the Spanish Civil War (1936–9), including many who were executed at the start of the conflict in Seville, Córdoba and Granada, which were among the first cities to be taken by Franco's Nationalist forces. One such victim was the Granada-born writer, Federico García Lorca. Indeed many artists, writers and intellectuals volunteered their support for the Republican cause, but they could not stand between Franco and a fascist victory.

Franco's Dictatorship

In the aftermath of World War II, in which Spain remained neutral, the country was left isolated and impoverished. Franco's dictatorship lasted until his death in 1975, a period of steady economic advance scarred by political and cultural repression. Many Andalusians migrated to the northern industrial cities or abroad, leaving the countryside deserted. Franco's acceptance in 1953 of American military bases in exchange for loans, along with Spain's subsequent admission to the UN, accelerated its economic recovery and led to the development of mass tourism during the 1960s.

In 1975, monarchy returned in the shape of King Juan Carlos, soon to be followed by democratic elections. In 1982 the Socialist PSOE party, led by the charismatic Sevillian lawyer Felipe González, won a sweeping victory that paved the way for long overdue investment in the region. The great manifestation of this was Expo '92 in Seville, which brought new roads, high-speed trains and a building boom to the regional capital.

And yet, for all the multimillion-peseta, high-tech facelifts, the romantic, rose-in-the-teeth view of Andalusia persists. The Andalusians themselves foster this image in their patios, bars, *peñas* (clubs) and *ferias* (fairs), and in the countryside, where donkeys are still used to plough the fields. Andalusia will always be Spain spiced with the tang of North Africa, a mountain-locked land racked by summer heat and fed by the waters of the Guadalquivir.

Above: a *tapas* bar in Seville, whose locals often encourage the rose-in-the-teeth image

HISTORY HIGHLIGHTS

circa **10000BC** Cave paintings at La Pileta (near Ronda) reveal presence of prehistoric settlers in Andalusia during Palaeolithic times.

2000–500 BC The kingdom of Tartessus flourishes in the area around Seville.

1100BC The Phoenicians found Gadir (Cádiz).

3rd century BC Carthaginian forces conquer Andalusia.

218BC Roman colonisation of Spain begins with the Second Punic War.

1st century BC–3rd century AD The Roman transformation of Andalusia develops agriculture and constructs roads and aqueducts. Itálica, Carmona and Seville are founded; Córdoba becomes the capital of Hispania Ulterior.

400–500 Spain is dominated by the Visigoths.

711 Moorish armies cross the Straits of Gibraltar; they conquer the peninsula within seven years.

756–1031 Umayyad dynasty rules over al-Andalus. Córdoba emerges as the capital of Muslim Spain; work starts on La Mezquita. In 929, Abd ar-Rahman III proclaims caliphate of Córdoba.

1086 The Almoravids, fundamentalist Muslim Berbers, invade Spain. They are expelled in 1147 by the Almohads, who build the Great Mosque of Seville, crowned by La Giralda minaret.

1212 The Almohads are defeated at the Battle of Las Navas de Tolosa. By 1248, Ferdinand III has taken Córdoba and Seville.

1237–1492 Nasrid dynasty rules the Kingdom of Granada. Construction of the Alhambra. In the 1360s Pedro the Cruel builds Seville's Alcázar; work starts on the cathedral in 1401.

1469 Marriage of Ferdinand V to Isabella I unites kingdoms of Aragón and Castile.

1492 Granada falls to Ferdinand and Isabella; Columbus discovers America.

1500s Seville granted trade monopoly with the New World. Various projects are initiated as a result of the ensuing prosperity. During the 1520s work begins on the cathedral in Córdoba's Mezquita, on Granada's cathedral, and on Charles V's palace in the Alhambra.

1600s The country's prosperity turns to decadence. Seville suffers a decline as the Guadalquivir silts up and trade moves to Cádiz. The city produces some of Spain's greatest artists.

1759–88 King Charles III introduces enlightened reforms; Seville's tobacco factory is completed.

1809–14 Seville, Córdoba and Granada are occupied by the French during the Peninsular War.

1800s Spain struggles to establish political stability and loses its colonies. The south of the country is discovered by Romantic writers and travellers.

1929 Ibero-American Exposition held in Seville.

1936–9 Spanish Civil War: Seville, Córdoba and Granada are occupied by Franco's Nationalists, parts of eastern Andalusia are held by Republicans.

1975 Franco dies; Juan Carlos I becomes king.

1982 The country votes into office a socialist government led by Sevillian Felipe González. Andalusia is granted new autonomous powers.

1986 Spain belatedly becomes a member of the European Union.

1992 Seville stages Expo '92. Celebrations mark the 500th anniversary of Columbus's discovery of America.

1999 Seville opens its new Olympic Stadium, built for its failed bid to host the 2004 Olympics. It does, though, host the World Athletics Championship.

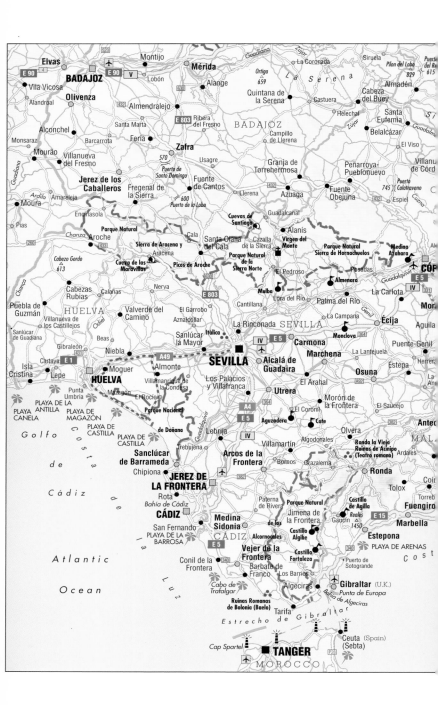

Itinerary 7
Itinerary 11
Itinerary 16

Andalusia

50 km / 30 miles

Seville

L et's build a church,' said the architects of Seville cathedral, 'so big that we shall be held to be insane.' And they did – a vainglorious feat that squats in the city centre like an obstinate bag-lady. The cathedral, with its great Moorish tower, La Giralda, is Seville's best known landmark, and worth the climb if only to orientate yourself in this jumble of narrow streets.

Seville has had a long-standing love affair with the grandiose. Next to the cathedral is Pedro the Cruel's splendid Alcázar, inspired by the Alhambra and enlarged by Charles V. To the south, the immense tobacco factory is second only to the Escorial in size. Beyond are the expansive remains of the pavilions, plazas and parks built for the 1929 Ibero-American Exposition.

The city also has an endearing panache, most obvious in its intense celebration of Semana Santa (Holy Week) and the subsequent Feria (April Fair). The style and energy of the Sevillian character came to the fore when the city became an international stage for Expo '92. The legacy of this investment bonanza can be seen in six new bridges, a new railway station, an expanded airport, a new theatre, restored museums and upgraded hotels. Yet it remains a quiet, intimate city, sensual and faintly decadent.

1. CATHEDRAL AND PARQUE DE MARIA LUISA
(see maps, p22&25)

Enjoy a short walking tour around the immense cathedral and ascend the Giralda (the cathedral's Moorish minaret), for a wonderful view of the city. After lunch, continue on foot to the venue of the 1929 Ibero-American Exposition, the Parque de María Luisa.

Breakfast in Seville tends to be a brisk, private affair – perhaps a *café con leche* (coffee with milk) and some *tostada* (toast) smeared with olive oil or fish paste. It's quite common for locals to eat breakfast standing at the bar, often in a mood of pensive solemnity. **Bar Los Principes** (Calle Arfe 7) evokes this mood admirably. By contrast, **Bar Ibense Bornay**, situated on the junction of Avenida de la Constitución and Calle Almirantazgo, is the ideal place for a quick *café* before you tackle Seville's cathedral.

The **Cathedral Santa María de la Sede** (Mon–Sat 11am–5pm, Sun 2–4pm)., which dates back to 1401, occupies the former site of a great mosque built by the Almohads in 1172. Indeed its gigantic proportions clearly reflect the Christian architects' ambition – to trump the grandeur of their 'heathen' predecessors. Of other cathedrals around the world, only St Paul's in London and St Peter's in Rome are larger. On arriving in Seville, you probably passed its rambling exterior and maybe noticed the enchained Roman

Left: the 600-year-old Cathedral Santa María de la Sede
Right: blowing the trumpet atop the Real Fábrica de Tabacos

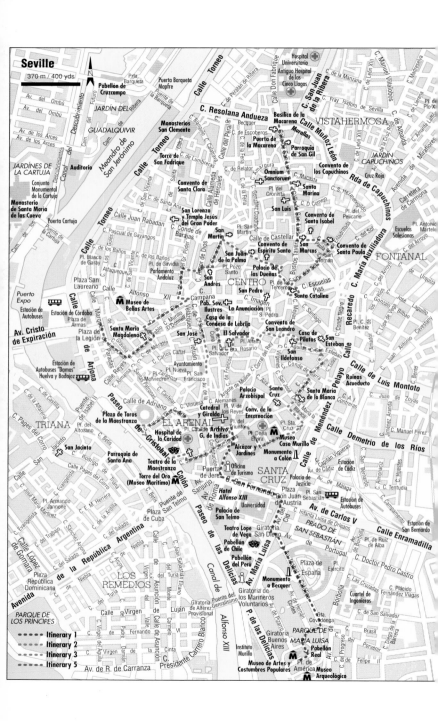

Seville

370 m / 400 yds

Itinerary 1
Itinerary 2
Itinerary 3
Itinerary 5

pillars, taken from Itálica, that surround it. The adjoining steps, **Las Gradas,** were for centuries Seville's main meeting-place. If you are crossing the street from the Bar Ibense Bornay, be sure to look up as you wait (and wait) for the traffic lights to change – you will have a clear view of **La Giralda** above the cathedral. Notice the silhouette of its crowning weather-vane (*giraldillo*), and a revolving bronze statue that represents Faith. This is not the original 16th-century statue, but a more recent copy.

There are several entrances to the cathedral. On the eastern side is the Puerta de Palos door, leading to the **Capilla Real** (Royal Chapel). The chapel is reserved for worshippers, as opposed to tourists, but there is nothing to stop you from taking a peek, as long as you are modestly dressed and observe a respectful silence. The area is cordoned off from the rest of the cathedral; the chapel itself is concealed behind a massive curtain. It is dedicated to the Virgen de los Reyes and contains a silver urn with the relics of King Ferdinand III (who expelled the Moors from Seville and Córdoba); nearby lie the resting places of his wife Beatrice and son Alfonso X (the Wise).

Leave the chapel and walk around the cathedral to the visitors' entrance. The entrance for tour groups is on the eastern side of the cathedral, and for individuals through the **Puerta del Perdón** on the northern side. Both lead into the **Patio de los Naranjos**, a courtyard lined with orange trees, a legacy of the original mosque. It seems inconceivable that this peaceful courtyard was a notorious sanctuary for criminals in the 16th century.

Gate of the Lizard

The **Puerta del Lagarto** (Gate of the Lizard, named after the life-sized wooden alligator that hangs incongruously from the ceiling) takes you into the cathedral's interior. Immediately to your left is the entrance to the Giralda, the original Moorish minaret which was capped with a Christian belfry, the ultimate *Reconquista* symbol. Climbing it is like watching a slide show of the city: 34 ramps and a flight of steps later you emerge beneath its awesome bells for a glorious view over Seville. Here you'll find not only a classic Andalusian skyline of white-washed houses and terracotta-tile roofs, for centuries pierced only by the domes and bell-towers of the city's churches and convents, but also the new-money monuments that have recently transformed the city. To the west, beyond the bullring, are the bridges built for Expo 92 (including the wishbone arch of the Puente de la Barqueta); to the east is the futuristic railway station, Santa Justa.

Return down the spiralling ramps of the Giralda. Dominating the scene

Right: the bells of La Giralda

ahead of you is the *coro* (choir) and **Capilla Mayor** (main chapel), while the depths of the cathedral's cavernous interior stretch to the right. Take a pew to study the Capilla Mayor's huge *retablo*, a deluge of gold that was begun in 1482 by the Flemish sculptor Pieter Dancar and not finished for a further 82 years. At the opposite side of the high altar from the gate by which you entered, inside the Puerta de San Cristóbal (completed in the early years of the 20th century) and usually surrounded by a small crowd of sightseers, you will spot the oversized tomb of Christopher Columbus, supported by four pallbearers representing the kingdoms of Castile, León, Aragón and Navarre.

Turn right here if you want to explore the incredible depths of the cathedral. Wandering on the outside of the choir, you are bound to be impressed by the cathedral's sheer enormity and scale. Notice the little side chapels, adorned

with statues and tombs, which are full of dusty corners that accommodate long-forgotten memorials. You will come to the **Sagrario**, the Tabernacle Chapel, which in effect is a church within a church. This is where large numbers of Sevillians attend Mass (access from the Avenida de la Constitución). At the far end of the cathedral is the huge, rarely opened **Puerta de la Asunción**.

Ecclesiastical Treasures

Backtrack past the Columbus tomb and towards the cathedral exit to inspect a series of side rooms that house ecclesiastical treasures. Beyond the chapel of Los Dolores is the **Sacristía de los Cálices**: amongst its many works of art you will encounter a common anachronistic depiction – this one by Goya – of the Giralda and two 3rd-

Above: the cathedral's Sacristía Mayor
Left: one of the cathedral's numerous art treasures

century Sevillian saints, Santa Justa and Santa Rufina, who escaped death in the lions' den. Next door is the **Sacristía Mayor** with more works by Zurbarán, Murillo and Van Dyck, along with some of the venerated relics that are paraded through the streets during Semana Santa. In the far corner of the cathedral, next to rooms exhibiting clerical vestments and illuminated manuscripts, a curved passage leads to the Sala Capitular, with an *Immaculate Conception* by Murillo.

After exploring the cathedral you'll be ready for lunch – head for the **Cervecería Giralda** (Calle Mateos Gago 1) opposite the cathedral exit, across the **Plaza Virgen de los Reyes**. If you arrive before 1.30pm you should be able to get a table in this busy *tapas* bar – look on the blackboard for the day's *raciones*. The menu normally includes typical Sevillian dishes such as *huevos a la flamenca* (eggs with ham and vegetables) and *cazuela Tío Pepe* (casserole cooked with sherry). For a more upmarket meal you might consider the **El Giraldillo** restaurant – it is touristy and expensive but the view from its tables is quite wonderful. Whatever you choose, do linger a moment in the Plaza de los Virgen Reyes – which is especially romantic at night when the light from its monumental lamppost illuminates the darkness.

Horse and Carriage Ride

In the afternoon you might amble towards the well-shaded bliss of the Parque de María Luisa. You can travel to the park in style by horse and carriage – there are several *coches de caballos* ranks around the cathedral. Negotiate a price before you set off. This will depend on how many passenters there are and how far you ride – official prices can be checked at the Tourist Office round the corner at Avenida de la Constitución 21. Otherwise

continue back towards the cathedral entrance, turning left into the Plaza del Triunfo, where a column celebrates the survival of the city in 1755, when an earthquake devastated Lisbon. Continue back to Avenida de la Constitución and turn left – en route you will pass the rear of the Lonja and the entrance to the Reales Alcázares (*see Itinerary 2, page 29*).

Avenida de la Constitución culminates in the Puerta de Jerez, and a veritable grand prix of traffic. Bear left around this roundabout to reach a luxury oasis, the **Hotel Alfonso XIII.** Opened in 1928, the hotel formed part of an ensemble of neo-Moorish, pro-Andalusian, *azulejo-* (glazed tile-) covered buildings that were constructed for the 1929 exposition. (A celebration

Seville Cathedral

50 m / 55 yds

- - - - **Itinerary 1**

Calle Alemanes

Placentines

Puerta del Perdón

Patio de los Naranjos

El Sagrario

Puerta de la Concepción

Puerta del Lagarto

Plaza Virgen de los Reyes

La Giralda

Puerta del Bautismo

Avenida de la Constitución

Puerta de Palos

Puerta de la Asunción

Coro

Capilla Mayor

Capilla Real

Puerta de la Natividad

Tomb of Christopher Columbus ★

Puerta de la Companilla

Sala Capitular

Puerta de San Cristóbal

Sacristía de los Calices

Sacristía Mayor

Plaza del Triunfo

of all things Spanish, and Spanish-American, Expo '29 took 15 years to create but ended in massive debt and anticlimax.) Have a drink in the bar and admire the hotel's grand patio.

Carmen was Here

Continue along Calle San Fernando to the great hulk of the **Real Fábrica de Tabacos** (tobacco factory), completed in 1757, and now part of Seville's university. You can walk through the building, which still bears signs of the days when thousands of young *cigarerras* rolled cigars here. The factory employed thousands of girls, who apparently piqued the interest of various foreign travellers, such as Prosper Mérimée, whose story about one of them inspired Bizet's opera *Carmen*.

Whether you walk through or round the building you will arrive at a junction with a statue of the *Reconquista* hero El Cid. Skirt round it, past the Teatro Lope de Vega and into the Avenida Isabel la Católica. The towers of the **Plaza de España**, inspired by the cathedral at Santiago de Compostela, will guide you.

The plaza once housed the Spanish Pavilion but is today a *azulejo*-crazed playground. The gardens of the **Parque de María Luisa**, where Romantic statuary pops up from the undergrowth, were once part of the grounds adjoining the baroque San Telmo Palace. Further south are two more pavilions in the Plaza de América *(see 'Museums' itinerary, page 33)*. When you are ready cut through to the riverside Paseo de las Delicias, where you can hail a taxi.

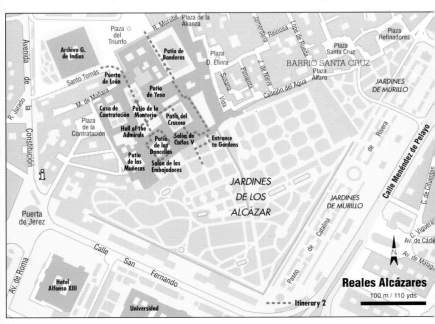

2. LA MAESTRANZA AND REALES ALCAZARES
(see maps, p22&26)

Visit the New World records office, the bullring and a 17th-century hospital built by the original Don Juan. After lunch, lose yourself in the magnificent Reales Alcazares (Royal Palaces) and its gardens.

The centre of Seville is neatly divided by the Avenida de la Constitución. To the east is the cathedral and the Barrio Santa Cruz – the old Jewish quarter that was refurbished in the 1920s and which has been metamorphosing into a picturesque tourist centre ever since. To the west lies El Arenal, a web of streets centred on Seville's bullring, La Maestranza.

Before exploring this area, you could visit the **Archivo General de Indias** (Mon–Fri 10am–1pm), in the heavyweight Lonja adjacent to the cathedral. Formerly the stock exchange building, the Lonja was designed in 1584 by Juan de Herrera, architect of Madrid's massive El Escorial. Since the 1750s it has been a records office for all the documents relating to the discovery and colonisation of the New World. A small number of the millions of papers stored here are on permanent display in the exhibition rooms up the grand stairs – you can see a street plan of Buenos Aires in 1713, a sketch of Inca weapons or a watercolour map of a fort in Florida.

Nuns' Cakes
From the Lonja cross over Avenida de la Constitución and turn right then left into Calle Almirantazgo. An archway to the right of the Café Los Pinelos leads into the little-visited **Plaza del Cabildo**, the scene of a collectors' market on Sundays. Look for a small shop, El Torno, which sells delicious cakes and biscuits baked by nuns from the various convents in and around Seville. This is a good place from which to buy something to nibble while visiting the Royal Palaces in the afternoon. From here you can take a passage into Calle Arfe.

Turn right, continuing down Calle Arfe and left into Calle Antonia Díaz. The easy-going eateries around the junction of streets here constitute a good selection of dinner options: straight ahead is the popular Mesón Sevilla Jabugo II and opposite a takeaway *freiduría* (fried fish shop – evenings only). Round the corner El Buzo and Bar Mesón Serranito serve Sevillian dishes in a bullfighters' ambience. Heading back towards the cathedral, Bodegas Diaz Salazar in Calle García de Vinuesa is friendly and authentic.

At the bottom of Calle Antonio Díaz is **La Maestranza** bullring (9.30am–2pm, 3–7pm) in the impressive **Plaza de Toros**. Built in 1760,

Above Left: Plaza de España, whose architects looked to Santiago de Compostela
Above: the Archivo General de Indias stores millions of historical documents

La Maestranza is one of the oldest, most prestigious bullrings in Spain. It's worth joining the 30-minute guided tour, which takes in the museum, matadors' chapel and stables.

From La Maestranza you can cross the road to the banks of the Río Guadalquivir, which was renamed the Canal de Alfonso XIII in 1948 when the river was diverted further west to prevent flooding. The river was re-opened for Expo '92, enabling visitors to cruise around the Isla de la Cartuja, the exhibition venue. Across the river to the north you'll see an iron bridge (built in 1852) crossing over to Triana, Seville's traditional gypsy quarter.

A blue-collar neighbourhood where Seville's dockers and stevedores lived, Triana has a different atmosphere from the rest of the city; it is particularly worth visiting for its shops, markets and lively bars.

Turn left to walk down the pleasant Paseo de Cristóbal Colón. Ahead is the 13th-century **Torre del Oro**, constructed by the Almohads to anchor an enormous chain that stretched across the river as part of the city's fortifications. Today it features a museum of nautical curiosities (Tues–Fri 10am–2pm, Sat and Sun 11am–2pm). Sightseeing bus tours of the city and cruises down the Guadalquivir leave from here.

Before you reach the tower cross the road and walk past the gardens of Seville's opera house, the **Teatro de La Maestranza** (Calle Nuñez de Balboa), which opened in 1991. At the end of the street is the **Hospital de la Caridad** (Mon–Sat 9am–1.30pm, 3.30–6.30pm). Founded in 1674, the building still functions as a charity hospital and is open to the public. In addition to its exquisite patio, it has a chapel (to the left) that exemplifies such institutions' great patronage of the arts during Seville's Golden Age. Among the works on display are ghoulish works by Valdés Leal (above the door and opposite) and paintings by Murillo.

Don Juan

On leaving the hospital you will see a statue of **Don Miguel de Mañara**, its founder, who is considered to be the role model for Don Juan, the cynical lover who apparently had 1,003 Spanish mistresses. The hospital became a point of call for Romantic writers and artists who believed Seville to be the hotbed of the lascivious south. Byron explained why in his own *Don Juan*:

> 'What men call gallantry, and gods adultery,
> Is much more common where the climate's sultry.'

Such matters might be discussed over a glass of *fino* in the cavernous **Bodegón Torre del Oro** round the corner (turn left into Calle Santander).

Above: in the Reales Alcazares, Pedro the Cruel's contribution to the city's majesty
Right: the dome over the Patio de las Doncellas

Suitably fortified, you are now in a position to take on the **Reales Alcazares** (Royal Palaces, winter: Tues–Sat 9.30am–6pm, Sun 9.30am–2.30pm; summer: Tues–Sat 9.30am–8pm, Sun 9.30am–6pm). The entrance is in the Plaza del Triunfo to the east of the cathedral – straight up Calle Santander and Calle Santo Tomás. The Reales Alcazares constitute Pedro the Cruel's contribution to Seville's majestic monuments. For a Castilian king (1350–69) with a reputation for barbaric behaviour, it is somewhat surprising to find in his palatial residences such a fulsome homage to the refined abstraction of Islam. Pedro, who adopted Arab dress and filled his court with Moorish entertainers, exemplifies the paradoxical affection the Reconquest monarchs seem to have felt for the culture they destroyed. Ironically he had little time to enjoy his Alcázar – he was murdered three years after its completion.

Enter through the **Puerta de León**, which is situated near some castellated walls left over from the Almohad fortress that previously stood here. Inside, you will quickly discover that the palaces have undergone considerable renovations since the 14th century. Passing through some small gardens you arrive in a large courtyard, the **Patio de la Montería**. Here you will find the work of Charles V, who added a whole set of **Royal Apartments** to the left. To the right is the **Casa de la Contratación**, an institution which, created by Ferdinand and Isabella, monopolised trade with the New World for over a century. Inside you'll find the **Hall of the Admirals**, where naval expeditions were planned, and a chapel with a starlit ceiling.

Pedro's Pleasure Dome

Ahead rises the exterior facade of Pedro's pleasure dome. Inside the dome, bear left, pass through a vestibule to enter its opulent centre, the **Patio de las Doncellas** (Maids' Courtyard). Much of the Alcázar's decoration was probably executed by the craftsmen who worked on Granada's magnificent Alhambra; Seville's Christian rulers allowed them to incorporate Koranic inscriptions into the intricate tiles and stucco work but had their own mottoes and coats of arms added. The upper storey is a 16th-century addition. The *azulejos* are the highlight of the impressive courtyard.

Continuing straight ahead you enter the **Salón de Carlos V** with its fine coffered ceiling. Turn right and you will find three rooms that once belonged to Pedro the Cruel's mistress, María de Padilla. Turn the corner for the **Salón**

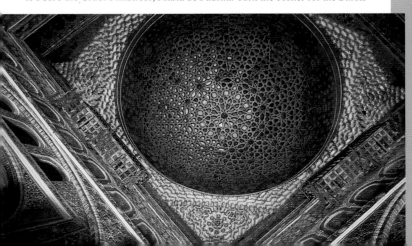

de los Embajadores (Ambassadors' Hall). The cedar cupola added in 1427 was restored and embellished in subsequent centuries, but the room, with its triple arcade of horseshoe arches, remains resoundingly Moorish. Parallel to this room is Philip II's dining room and bedroom. The sober wooden ceiling of the latter forms a contrast to the starbursts elsewhere.

Next you enter the **Patio de las Muñecas** (Dolls' Courtyard) which was apparently named after a pair of minute doll's heads that appear in the ornamentation. The upper floor is a mid-19th century 'enhancement'. To the left is Isabella the Catholic's bedroom, and ahead that of her only son, Don Juan. To the right is the **Salón de los Reyes Moros** (Hall of Moorish Kings).

Renaissance Japery

Back in the Patio de la Montería turn right towards an arcade. To the left of this you will find the oldest section of the Alcázar: here is the **Patio de Yeso** that was originally part of the 12th-century Almohad palace. Continue through the gardens to the **Charles V Apartments**. The first of these is a room full of Flemish tapestries that depict the bellicose Charles's military campaigns in Tunisia. The apartments also feature the Emperor's Hall and Chapel. Here the bright yellow *azulejos*, bursting with avaricious birds, snake-entwined cherubs and general Renaissance japery, make a refreshing change from the meditative geometrics of Islamic interior design. The *azulejos'* light-heartedness forms an ideal introduction to the Alcázar's gardens that follow – a rambling paradise of box hedges and citrus groves punctuated with assorted pools, pavilions and fountains.

3. City Walk via Casa de Pilatos *(see map, p22)*

An afternoon stroll through the some of the city's prettiest backstreets, visiting the Casa de Pilatos and culminating in the shops of Calle Sierpes. Start at about 4pm on a weekday to arrive in Sierpes when the 'paseo'

is in full swing and its shops and cafés are bubbling with life.

Starting in the **Patio de las Banderas** (Courtyard of Flags), take the Reales Alcázares exit. An archway in the far corner will lead you into the narrow streets of the **Barrio Santa Cruz**. Passing the covered alley, bear left into Calle Vida. Leave via the long Callejón del Agua which ends in the Plaza de Alfaro: steps to the right lead down to the **Jardines de Murillo**

(Murillo Gardens). Continue ahead, bearing left into the Plaza de Santa Cruz, framed by Sevillian mansions and with a 17th-century iron cross in the centre. Further on, Calle Mezquita takes you to the Plaza Refinadores (Polishers' Square), overseen by a haughty statue of Don Juan.

Look for a small alley – Calle Mariscal – that will take you up to the Plaza de Cruces (Square of Crosses) and another square. At the top turn right into Calle Ximénez de Enciso, at the end of which turn left towards the Hotel Fernando III for Calle Cespedes. This road wends its way to Calle Levies, where you will be confronted by a huge red-brick building (once a noble house, then a convent and now a government building). Bear left into the Plaza de las Mercedarias, then take Calle Vidrio until it becomes pedestrianised, turning left (by No 25) into a tiny alley, the Calle Cristo del Buen Viaje. This delivers you to Calle San Esteban. Turn left towards the restful **Plaza de Pilatos**, where a statue of the great painter Zurbarán will greet you.

Arab Artistry, Italian Grace

The **Casa de Pilatos** (daily 9am–6pm, 8pm in summer) is said to have been modelled on Pontius Pilate's house in Jerusalem by its creator, the Marquis of Tarifa. Completed in 1540, it is decorated in Mudéjar style but has none of the introversion and claustrophobia found in Pedro the Cruel's earlier Alcázar. Spacious and eclectic, it is a delightul combination of Italianate grace and Arab artistry. You enter first through a Roman-style triumphal arch, crossing the *apeadero* (carriage yard) to its central patio where arcades of Moorish arches are echoed by Gothic arches on the floor above.

This courtyard contains some of the finest *azulejos* you are likely to see: dazzling, puzzle-book patterns in brilliant colours that include extraordinary, quasi-Impressionist designs. The Roman statuary was imported from Italy. Walk to the right, through the Praetorian Chamber, to find a small garden. Continuing around the patio in an anti-clockwise direction, you will encounter the chapel and Pilate's study, which open onto enchanting gardens blessed with trickling fountains and cascading bougainvillea. A monumental staircase

Above Left: the Charles V Apartments are full of colourful *azulejos*
Left: timepieces for sale in Barrio Santa Cruz. **Above:** inside the Casa de Pilatos

leads to a late Mudéjar cupola (1537). You can take a rather abrupt guided tour of the upstairs apartments, which are packed with art treasures acquired over the centuries by the palace's aristocratic owners; parts of the house are still used for domestic purposes by the Medinaceli family.

When you leave, turn right to walk past the Hostal Atenas (Calle Caballerizas) to reach the ochre and amber facade of the baroque Iglesia de San Ildefonso. Directly opposite is a brown metal door that leads into the **Convento San Leandro**, a closed-order convent where you can buy – via a brass-studded revolving drum – its famous *yemas* (*see 'Heavenly Sweets' in Eating Out, page 70*).

Shopping Centre

Leave the adjacent plaza by the far corner, where Calle Boteros then Calle Odreros wind through to the **Plaza Alfalfa**, scene of a pet market on Sunday mornings. If you're peckish, the **Horno San Buenaventura** patisserie is heaven for cake-lovers. From here you can follow the narrow Calle Alcaicería de la Loza (by the Carlos Antigüedades shop) into the city's most extensive pedestrian shopping area. First is the **Plaza de Jesús de la Pasión**, devoted to wedding-dress shops, followed by the popular **Plaza del Salvador**. Between the two sits the Church of El Salvador, built mostly during the 17th century.

The Plaza del Salvador sits halfway up a length of shopping streets running north–south. For a good circuit of the shops, walk up to the top of Calle de la Cuna, turn left and then return down the city's main strolling and spending artery, Calle Sierpes. While passing along Calle de la Cuna look out for the **Palacio de la Condesa de Lebrija** (at No 8;

Top: the Plateresque facade of the old town hall
Above: a sharp operator on the street

Mon–Fri 11am–1pm, 5–7pm, Sat 10am–1pm), another Sevillian stately home with a grand patio and stunning mosaics filched from Itálica. At the top of Calle Sierpes, La Campana (No 1) is one of the best cake shops in Spain. At the southern end of the street is the **Plaza Nueva** and the Plateresque facade of the old **Ayuntamiento** (Town Hall, 1564); beyond is the Avenida de la Constitución and the cathedral.

For dining consider the restaurants clustered around the north end of Calle Sierpes. Among these is **Las Columnas de Baco** (Calle Santa María de Gracía 2; tel: 954 224320), especially recommended if you want to escape the grime of the streets; it's significantly cheaper to eat at the bar than at a table. Back in the Plaza del Salvador the **Bar Alicantina** is famous for its seafood *tapas*, while on the opposite end of the square bars such as La Antigua Bodeguita and Los Soportales cater to a young crowd.

4. MUSEUMS *(see map, p22)*

A round-up of Seville's best museums.

Entrance to the following museums is free to citizens of EU countries.

The **Museo de Bellas Artes** (Plaza del Museo; Tues 3–8pm; Wed–Sat 9am–8pm, Sun 9am–2pm) is the city's premier museum. For years it was closed for restoration, the completion of which was hastened by Expo '92. The building, constructed as the Convento de la Merced Calsada by Juan Oviedo in 1612, has three patios bordered by two floors of galleries that exhibit works from medieval times onwards. The main convent chapel's baroque ceiling is so gloriously coloured that it competes with the works below. Look out for the Seville School's religious paintings and sculptures, commissioned by the city's abundant convents, monasteries and hospitals. The artists include El Greco, Pacheco, Velázquez, Zurbarán, Leal, Murillo… Also worth seeing are vistas of the Guadalquivir with steamships docked beside the Torre del Oro and Gonzalo Bilbao's 1915 tribute to the tobacco factory workers: *Las Cigarerras.*

There are two museums on the Plaza de América at the southern end of the Parque de María Luisa. The **Museo de Artes y Costumbres Populares** (Mudéjar Pavilion Tues 3–8pm, Wed–Sat 9am–8pm, Sun 9am–2pm), featuring costumes, portraits and agricultural oddities, offers insights into the traditions of Andalusia. Opposite, is the **Museo Arqueológico** (Tues 3–8pm; Wed–Sat 9am–8pm, Sun 9am–2pm), containing the Tartessian Carambolo Treasure. This collection covers neolithic to Moorish times and includes Roman mosaics and statues from Itálica and Ecija.

MUSEO DE BELLAS ARTES

Right: the Museo de Bellas Artes

5. CHURCHES *(see map p22)*

A long walk through the backstreets of the Barrio Macarena – the 'Soul of Seville' – to the Basilica de Macarena, past some of the finest churches.

In the centre of the Plaza de Armas, the **Old Córdoba Railway Station** (1889) is a fine example of Sevillian architecture that served as a reference point for the future styles of regionalism and modernism. Having housed the Sevillian Pavilion in Expo '92, it is now an up-market commercial centre.

With the river at your back, walk to the next corner (Calle Marqués de Paradas) and turn right. When the road splits, bear left along Calle Julio César and continue until the Calle Reyes Católicos. Turn left and the street narrows. If you look above the buildings you will glimpse the colourful cupola of the church of **Santa María Magdalena**. It is difficult to see the building clearly because of the trees but it is worth looking for an angle to do so.

Past the church, turn left onto Calle Bailén then right at the next small plaza, which has lots of interesting buildings, into the shopping street Calle San Eloy. You might stop for a coffee at the **Cafe Zafiro** in the plaza or a *tapa* at the **Bar Rincón San Eloy** (No 30). Continuing to the end of the street, turn left into the small garden square of Plaza del Duque de la Victoria, which hosts a pleasant 'hippy market' (Thur, Fri, Sat). For more serious shopping, try the El Corte Inglés department store. Leave the plaza with El Corte Inglés on your left and walk along Calle Jesús del Gran Poder, past the Plaza de la Concordia.

In front of the Farmacia Militar, turn right into Calle San Miguel then left when you reach Calle Amor de Dios, a street which seems to be an endless showcase of Sevillian urban architecture. Immediately turn right into **Calle San Andrés** and the small, mostly Gothic church of **San Andrés**. Leave by Calle Cervantes, passing under the ceramic 'street chapel' of Nuestro Padre Jesús del Gran Poder. Ahead is the 14th-century Gothic church of **San Martín**. Leave the Plaza San Martín by way of Calle Viriato. Some 100 metres/yds away is the Gothic-Mudéjar church of **San Juan de la Palma**, finished in 1788; notice the baroque bell tower and the unusual rectangular stained-glass window over the entrance. To the right is the Renaissance facade of an old seignorial house which is now a shop.

From the plaza you can see the bell tower of the **Convento de Espíritu Santo**. Continue along the Calle San Juan de la Palma and follow the convent wall into Calle Dueñas until you reach the entrance to the **Palacio de las Dueñas**, a palace owned by the Duchess de Alba. It isn't open to visitors but if the gate is ajar you might catch a glimpse of the garden.

Take Calle Doña Maria Coronel then the first left, Calle Gerona. If hungry, try the El Rinconcillo café (No 32) before reaching the Mudéjar doorway of the church of **Santa Catalina**. Inside, note the Portal Gótico, the Mudéjar details and the tower. Turn left towards the Plaza de los Terceros then keep right at the **Libreria-Anticuaria Los Terceros**. About 50 metres (165ft) further along on the right is the 17th-century church of **Los Terceros**. The colonial baroque entrance at the back of the church dates from the 18th century.

At the **Plaza de San Román** is another Gothic-Mudéjar church. Take the left side of the church along Calle de Enladrillada. At the beginning of a long white wall turn left into Calle Santa Paula. At the plaza beyond you will find the **Convento de Santa Paula**. If you arrive during the posted visiting hours, knock on the right hand door. A nun will show you around the museum and offer to sell you some home-made sweets and marmalades.

Leave the plaza by way of Calle Santa Paula (which becomes Calle Los Siete Dolores de Nuestra Señora). **Plaza Santa Isabel**, although at times dirty, is good place from which to admire the Renaissance facade of the huge church of the **Convento de Santa Isabel** before visiting the smaller Church of **San Marcos** beside the square. The church tower was once a mosque minaret; the Mudéjar windows date back at least to the 14th century.

The Most Beloved Virgin

Facing the church's main door, turn left and follow Calle de San Luis. Soon you will see, on the left, the three doors of the **Iglesia de San Luis** (1699), one of the best examples of Sevillian baroque. Continuing along Calle de San Luis pass the small church of **Santa Marina** to the right and the **Parroquia de Gil** before arriving at the **Puerta de la Macarena**, the gate in the old Islamic walls. Next to the gate, the **Basilica de la Macarena** was built in 1949 as a church-museum to house Seville's most beloved Virgin – **La Esperanza-Macarena**. For a small fee you can see the statue, which leaves its pedestal only during Holy Week, when it is paraded through the streets.

Across the road from the basilica is the delightfully old-fashioned **Bar Plata**. Around the corner from here is the massive **Hospital de las Cinco Llagas**, which is now home to the regional parliament.

Left: inside the Convento de Santa Paula
Above: one of the Church of San Marcos's Mudéjar windows

seville itineraries

6. THE ISLA CARTUJA *(see map, p22)*

Expo '92 left an indelible impression on Seville, with its most visible legacy being architectural. The site itself, situated on the island of Cartuja, continues to attract visitors to its diverse range of attractions.

In 1992 Seville hosted the World Fair, Expo '92. To facilitate such a prestigious event, the city had to undergo a thorough transformation and a whole new town of pavilions and exhibition spaces was built on a 182-hectare

(450-acre) site on the island of Cartuja. The event attracted more than 41 million visitors and placed Seville firmly on the international map. Ten years later, the city is still appreciating the side-effects of this grand project. Various innovative bridges were built to span the Guadalquivir, notably the wishbone-shaped Puente de la Barqueta and the harp-like Puente del Alamillo. The city also benefits from a revamped airport, a new railway station, new roads and designer hotels.

A number of Expo '92's bold, high-tech pavilions have survived on Cartuja. Some of these buildings now form part of a Science and Technology Park, while others are utilised by the city's university. The island's restored 14th-century **Monasterio de Santa María de la Cueva** (Tues–Sat 10am–8pm, Sun 10am–3pm), which was used as the Royal Pavilion during Expo '92, was once a home from home for Christopher Columbus. The great explorer's grave was located here for a time. Between 1841 and 1980 the monastery housed the Pickman ceramics factory, which was known for its Cartuja porcelain. Part of the monastery now incorporates the **Centro Andaluz de Arte Contemporáneo**, Seville's modern art museum.

New World Theme Park

Further north along the banks of the Guadalquivir, some 34 hectares (85 acres) of the Cartuja island are given over to the delights of the **Isla Mágica** theme park (Mar–Oct: daily, all day). The theme in this case is the conquest of the New World, with the accent firmly on street entertainment. The park also features plenty of appropriately hair-raising white-knuckle rides.

Other attractions on the island include the **Auditorio de La Cartuja**, an open-air auditorium that seats 11,000 spectators for its occasional performances, and the **Teatro Central**, a modern theatre that regularly stages plays, concerts and dance performances. The northern part of the island features the large, leafy **Parque El Alamillo**. Of more recent vintage, the 60,000-seat **Estadio Olímpico** was built as part of the city's unsuccessful bid to host the 2004 Olympic Games. The stadium served as the venue for the 1999 World Athletics Championships.

Above: thrills and spills at the Isla Mágica theme park
Right: church in the hamlet of El Rocío on the edge of the Doñana Park

Excursion

7. THE DONANA NATIONAL PARK *(see map p18–19)*

Spreading over 500sq km (190sq miles) at the mouth of the Guadalquivir, the Doñana National Park is one of Europe's great natural treasures. This excursion takes in the park tour, with stops at the wine-making town of Bollullos, the shrine of El Rocío, and the port from which Columbus launched his famous voyage of discovery to the New World.

This excursion can be easily travelled in a day but if you join the morning tour the best option is to spend the previous night in El Rocío.

The **Doñana National Park** can be visited only on the official tour, in specially adapted four-wheel-drive vehicles. Departing from the park's main visitors centre in El Acebuche in Huelva province, the tour lasts four hours. There is one tour in the morning and another in the afternoon every day except Sunday during summer, and every day except Monday during the rest of the year. To book a place, contact the Cooperativa Marismas del Rocío (tel: 959 430 432). Winter and spring are the best times to visit; in summer, especially in years when there has been little rainfall, the marshes can dry up.

The Largest Winery

Take the E-1 motorway west towards Huelva. After 51km (30 miles) you reach the turning for **Bollullos Par del Condado**, the principal town in the Condado de Huelva wine-growing area, which produces crisp whites, nutty *olorosos* and *finos* – a sort of rustic sherry. You could stop at the Casa del Vino at the town entrance to sample the local brew. To visit the Bodegas Andrade, the town's largest private winery, call ahead (tel: 959 410 106).

Leave Bollullos on the A-483 road, which takes you past the farming town of Almonte to the hamlet of **El Rocío**, on the edge of the Doñana Park. For most of the year, the place seems eerily deserted, but for three days in

spring it becomes the spiritual centre of Andalusia. This is when approximately a million pilgrims congregate for the annual Romería del Rocío fiesta, arriving by car, bus or, more traditionally, in ox-drawn carriages, on horseback or even on foot. The centre of attention is a small image of the Virgin Mary that was discovered here by a hunter from Almonte 700 years ago. You can visit the shrine where the famous image is kept.

El Rocío is a good base from which you can branch out if you are spending the night. Stay at the hamlet's unpretentious and friendly Hotel Toruño (tel: 959 442 323), some of whose rooms overlook the Doñana marshes, or at the slightly more expensive Cortijo Los Mimbrales (tel: 959 442 237), which offers comfortable lodgings in the midst of a citrus farm 1km (1½ mile) south of El Rocío. Two kilometres (1¼ miles) south of El Rocío is the La Rocina visitors centre, where you can pick up maps and brochures. A detour of 5km (3 miles) takes you to the **Palacio de Acebrón**, an incongruous and sinister-looking neoclassical palace at the park's edge. From here, an interesting, shaded and easy hiking path runs alongside the Acebrón stream.

The Elusive Lynx

Back on the main road, continue south for another 12km (7 miles) to reach **El Acebuch**e, the park's central reception centre and tour starting point. The Doñana park is a vital refuge for countless birds that migrate between Europe and Africa each year; some species spend the winter here, others nest in the park's marshlands.

But the most emblematic denizen of the park is the extremely rare Spanish lynx, the most endangered animal species in Europe. These nocturnal, prowling felines inhabit the thick underbrush of the upper reaches of the park. Sighting the elusive lynx is a rare experience indeed, even for the naturalists who work here permanently. You are more likely to spot wild boar and deer.

The tour covers around 70km (40 miles) and, though it takes in only a fraction of the park, it is enough to give you a good idea of the various habitats that exist here. You will be driven along sandy white beaches pounded by the Atlantic surf as far as the mouth of the Guadalquivir, before plunging into the park's flat marshlands. Next you travel through forests of umbrella pines to reach a landscape of sand dunes. These shifting waves of sand, constantly, if imperceptibly, on the move, engulf copses of pine trees. As the sands move on, only the trees are left behind, like weird natural sculptures starkly silhouetted.

If you have time, you might want to extend your visit to the region to

Left: traditional dress in El Rocío

take in the towns that played a part in Columbus's historic voyage in 1492. Heading south from El Acebuche, skirting the ugly high-rise holiday resort of Matalascañas, the road travels through pine forests to reach Mazagón, a quiet seaside village with a fine *parador* (tel: 959 536 300).

La Rábida Monastery

After 11km (7 miles) you will find the 15th-century Franciscan monastery of **La Rábida**, where Columbus showed up in 1485 in search of refuge and a sympathetic ear for his proposal. This he found in the figure of Fray Juan Perez, the former confessor to the Spanish queen. Today the monastery – which features a Mudéjar-style inner courtyard, a 14th-century church and the Sala Capitular, where Columbus planned the final arrangements for his voyage – makes for an interesting visit, on a guided tour conducted by a monk.

On the coast not far from the monastery is the **Muelle de las Carabelas**, which is a reconstruction of a 15th-century port complete with full-scale replicas of the three ships, the *Niña*, the *Pinta* and the *Santa María*, that delivered Columbus and his crew to the New World.

In the neighbouring town of **Palos de la Frontera**, where Columbus signed up most of his crew, you can see La Fontanilla, the fountain from which the famous flotilla extracted enough water to last the long journey across the Atlantic. It was from Palos's port that the flotilla sailed down the Río Tinto river to the ocean just before sunrise on 3 August 1492. In the intervening centuries the river changed course and today the town is landlocked.

Return to Seville by an alternative route, rejoining the E-1 motorway 18km (11 miles) from the town, heading east. Seville is a further 80km (50 miles) away. On the way it is worth stopping at the medieval town of **Niebla**, 2km (1¼ mile) off the main road, whose fortifications are particularly impressive. Two kilometres (1¼ miles) of walls, with five fine gateways, encircle the old part of town. Within, you can visit the 15th-century Castillo de los Guzmán, before heading back to Seville.

Above: a section of the Doñana National Park

Córdoba

Córdoba hugs a lazy bend of the Guadalquivir at the southern foot of the Sierra Morena, 140km (87 miles) east of Seville. For a city with such a glorious past – it was the capital of Roman Spain and then later of al-Andalus – Córdoba is surprisingly provincial. The city's enduring attraction is the vast, innovative mosque constructed by the Moors on the north bank of the river between the 8th and 11th centuries: La Mezquita – one of the wonders of the world. The city's old quarter fans out around this landmark into a compact warren of whitewashed houses, winding alleys and flower-filled patios. There are several small hotels, plus cheaper *hostales* and *pensiones*, often with patios, in the old quarter. If you don't mind sacrificing a degree of comfort for some authentic regional character, these accommodation options are for the most part recommended. Alternatively, for the luxuries supplied by cosmopolitan hotels, check out the range of choices in the modern city that sprawls beyond the old quarter.

8. LA MEZQUITA *(see maps, p43 &45)*

La Mezquita is best visited in the early evening when the sun has warmed its ancient stones and the school groups and armed guards have gone. Spend the morning exploring the labyrinthine old quarter or visiting the Alcázar or Palacio de Viana (see Itinerary 9, page 46).

Allow two hours for a visit to the mosque (especially if you appreciate good architecture), and bring a jacket because it tends to be very cool inside.

Before you set out consider calling **El Caballo Rojo** (Cardenal Herrero 28, tel: 957 475 375), the most famous restaurant in Córdoba, to book a table for dinner. It specialises in *antigua cocina mozarabe* (traditional Córdoban dishes spiced and sweetened with Moorish flavours) such as *cordero al miel* (lamb in honey) and *revuelto siglo XI* (scrambled egg à la 11th century).

Begin in the **Patio de los Naranjos**, which you can enter from either the east or the west side of the Mezquita. An enclosed garden with bubbling fountains and lines of orange trees, it is an ideal place in which to sit and get your bearings. Construction of **La Mezquita** (summer: 10am–7pm; winter: 10am–5pm) began in AD785, two decades after Abd ar-Rahman I, founder of the Umayyad dynasty, declared himself emir

Left: the Roman bridge from Torre de la Calahorra
Right: one of several entrances to La Mezquita

of al-Andalus. Until then Córdoba's Moorish and Christian communities had shared the site's Visigothic church, San Vicente, which was partitioned into two parts. After purchasing the Christian half of the church, the Moors built a new mosque, using the old buildings materials. The mosque occupied only a quarter of today's site.

Over the course of the next two centuries, as Córdoba's wealth and prestige grew, successive rulers enlarged and embellished this original structure, extending the mosque east and as far south as the Guadalquivir allowed. In 1236, when Ferdinand III captured Córdoba, the Mezquita reverted to Christian ownership: Catholic chapels were established between the Roman and Visigothic pillars and many of its entrances were blocked.

In the 16th century an extravagant cathedral was erected here, to the chagrin of Charles V, who said: 'You have built here something you could have built anywhere, but you have destroyed what was unique in the world.' This was rather ironic given that Charles had made his own 'improvements' to both the Alhambra and Seville's Alcázar, and that it was Charles who sanctioned the work in the first place.

Mental Manoeuvres

An appreciation of the Mezquita's former glory therefore requires some deft mental manoeuvres and the subtraction of the Christian appendages. First remove the closed arches along the mosque's northern wall, then open all the doors in the walls surrounding the patio. Now lose the 16th-century bell-tower encasing the original minaret, swap the orange trees for olive trees, palms and cypresses, and lastly add a well and a water-wheel to the fountains.

In Arab cities a mosque is less a private religious compound than an integral part of the neighbourhood; it is a combination of thoroughfare, meeting place and, at the appointed hours, a place of communal prayer. The patio functioned as a courtyard for ritual ablution before prayer, the faithful being summoned by the wailing call from its slender minaret. Its main entrance would have been the **Puerta del Perdón** adjacent to this tower, which lies parallel to the principal entrance to the mosque, the **Puerta de las Palmas** (next to the four naves with wooden lattices).

The Mezquita's Stone Magic

Palm trees, Arabian tents, Roman aqueducts, fans, acrobats on each other's shoulders ... theories abound as to what inspired the Mezquita's architects to create the innovative pillar-and-arch design that makes Córdoba's mosque such a thrill. What is clear is that they began with a pile of assorted columns and capitals gathered from the earlier Visigothic church and other plundered sources in the area around al-Andalus. The builders may also have kept one of the Visigothic church walls in place – a possible explanation for the Mezquita's great mystery: why does the *qibla* (prayer wall), which traditionally faces east to Mecca, actually face south?

These columns, all of differing height and stone, were ingeniously incorporated into the building – sunk into the ground, raised up, inverted – and then topped by other columns. Two tiers of arches, constructed of red brick and white plaster, then bridged the gap between them – the higher arch supporting the roof, the lower strengthening the grid of columns. The result is apparently top-heavy, but when repeated row upon row, it creates a momentum and harmony that is ultimately spacious and agile. Later architects elaborated on this basic form by interlacing and poly-lobing (an effect resembling a bite-mark) the arches. The result, built more than 1,000 years before Escher's visual conundrums and the world of computer graphics, is stone magic.

Above Right: Mezquita columns and arches

córdoba itineraries

Both gates were redecorated in the Mudéjar style but Puerta de las Palmas is still flanked by two Roman columns and a plaque inscribed in Arabic. In the manner of an architect's sign, the plaque states that, in the Muslim year 346, Abd ar-Rahman commissioned Said ben-Ayub to build the mosque.

Entering La Mezquita

Today you enter the hall of the mosque through a small door on the patio's southeast corner. Before resuming this itinerary in the far corner to your right (by the wooden lattices), you will probably want to explore the mosque at your leisure for a little while.

What little illumination there is shines above a lonely Visigothic font that, by the end of the day, is usually full of empty film canisters. This corner of the Mezquita is the original rectangle built by Abd ar-Rahman I. Along the walls, rows of Catholic chapels stretch into the gloom. Remove these and you can imagine how the serried pillars within the mosque formed a continuation of the trees back in the Patio de los Naranjos. This was part of a subtle transition from the mundane to the divine that culminates in the *mihrab*, the sacred niche in the prayer wall where the Koran is kept.

Walking ahead in an anti-clockwise direction you will find yourself in the mosque's first extension, which was added by Abd ar-Rahman II in 833.

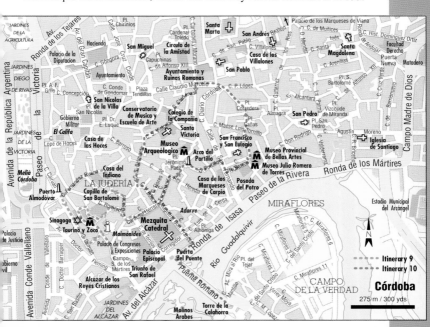

(A slight ramp in the floor is evidence of the extension.) To the left is the rear of the cathedral *coro* (choir). Further on is the vaulted ceiling of an aborted attempt to build a church here in the 15th century. To the left you will see the domed **Capilla de Villaviciosa** where the old mosque's *mihrab* would have been. Through a cutaway you can see the **Capilla Real** next door, redecorated in the 14th century in Mudéjar stucco. This was the mosque's *maqsura* (royal enclosure).

Continuing ahead you enter the Mezquita's major enlargement, a legacy of the golden days of 10th-century Córdoba. This was constructed in 964 by al-Hakam II, son of the self-proclaimed Caliph Abd ar-Rahman III. He pushed the southern wall right up to the river and built a new opulent *mihrab*, decorated with dazzling mosaics and an influential, star-ribbed dome that was subsequently copied throughout Spain. This lies beyond a set of railings – the bejewelled side-chambers formed the *maqsura*. Domed skylights had to be introduced at this stage due to the distance from the light of the patio.

The Triumph of Efficiency

Turning left, pass the cathedral sacristy and enter the **third extension** of the Mezquita, built by the belligerent al-Mansur in 990 to accommodate Córdoba's growing population. With the Alcázar to the west and the river to the south, his only option was to extend eastwards, widening both the hall and courtyard. Here the construction was conducted with more efficiency than artistry: the capitals of its uniform columns are less elaborate, the

arches' red colouring is merely superficial paintwork. These aesthetic short-comings are probably a reflection of al-Mansur's priorities: his main interest was in extending his caliphate, which reached Santiago da Compostela.

Beside you stands the towering Christian **Cathedral**. The construction of this stunning building began in 1523 and took two centuries to complete. With its narrow aisles and lofty **Capilla Mayor**, deliberately designed to humble worshippers and direct their eyes up towards the heavens, the cathedral stands in marked contrast to the Mezquita and its less hierarchical ethos. Among the cathedral's numerous fine features, a highlight is the carved mahogany choir stalls that fill the *coro* like some elaborate confection in dark chocolate, and the magnificent golden altarpiece containing 36 tableaux of the Life of Christ.

Returning to the outside world, take the western exit from the Patio de los Naranjos and walk south towards the river. Here you will pass the richest of the Mezquita's facades. The first doorway you enounter, St. Stephen's, was the original entrance to both the Visigothic church and Abd ar-Rahman I's original mosque. Next you pass the extension by Abd ar-Rahman II and another door, St. Michael's, that would have been a royal passageway from the Alcázar to the mosque's *maqsura*.

There are three other entrances to La Mezquita, all with brass-faced doors, that date to the al-Hakam II period. Look out for the central entrance which, with its gothic arch stuck like a pointed hat on top of the previous Moorish horseshoe, neatly encapsulates the spirit of architectural oneupmanship that has created the Mezquita you see today.

The prevailing principle when looking at the Mezquita is to realise that, throughout the complex, the preservation of historical artefacts has been at the expense of aesthetic considerations. Nowhere is this truth better witnessed than in the Mezquita's southwestern corner. Here you will find a wild collision of time's leftovers: a Roman bridge, a 16th-century triumphal gate built by Philip II and an 18th-century monumental column dedicated to St Raphael.

For an Evening Stroll

For much of the day these edifices are spoilt by the noise, fumes and pollution of the local traffic. Once the Mezquita closes, however, the city suddenly relaxes. This is the ideal time for taking a constitutional stroll across the Puente Romano. Pause beside the silty waters of the Guadalquivir and, like so many before you, contemplate Córdoba in the fading sunlight, before preparing yourself for dinner (*see Eating Out, page 72*).

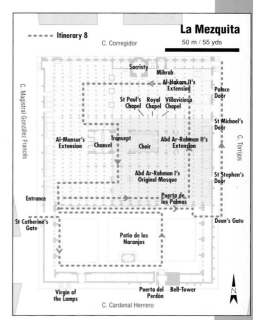

La Mezquita

- - - - Itinerary 8   C. Corregidor   50 m / 55 yds

Sacristy
Mihrab
Al-Hakam II's Extension
Palace Door
St Paul's Chapel   Royal Chapel   Villaviciosa Chapel
St Michael's Door
C. Magistral González Francés
Al-Mansur's Extension   Transept   Abd Ar-Rahman II's Extension
Chancel   Choir
C. Torrijos
Abd Ar-Rahman I's Original Mosque
St Stephen's Door
Entrance
Puerta de las Palmas
St Catherine's Gate
Dean's Gate
Patio de los Naranjos
Virgin of the Lamps   Puerta del Perdón   Bell-Tower
C. Cardenal Herrero
N

Above Left: Moorish influences
Left: cupola above the *mihrab*

9. EXPLORING THE JUDERÍA *(see map, p43)*

Córdoba's old Jewish quarter, the Judería, is situated to the northwest of the Mezquita, and can be explored in a couple of hours.

A Jewish community has resided in this quarter since Roman times. In the subsequent era, persecution by the Visigoths persuaded the Jews to side with the invading Moors. As a reward for their support, the Jews were permitted to remain in the city. For seven centuries they lived in generally fruitful coexistence with Córdoba's tolerant Muslim rulers, until Ferdinand and Isabella's edict of expulsion forced them out in 1492.

The quarter is now a relaxed maze of narrow streets whose smarter residences and dilapidated historic buildings have been infiltrated by craft shops and souvenir stalls. Start in the **Calle Cardenal Herrero** and walk west towards a T-junction of streets that look like open markets. Here you will find the tempting Helados Alberti ice cream parlour. Take a sharp right down Calle Deanes, on which you should look out for No 16, which has a selection of the *filigrana de plata* (silver filigree) for which Córdoba has long been famous. You can buy cassettes of flamenco and guitar music around here.

At the end of the street turn left into Calle Buen Pastor, which curls uphill to the Plaza Angel Torres. Nearby is the **Casa del Indiano**, a misleading name for a 15th-century Mudéjar-style gate. Walk past this portal and you will reach the more substantial **Puerta Almodóvar**, part of the Moorish city walls. If you turn left beyond this (after a deferential bow in the direction of the statue of the Roman writer Seneca), you can follow a pleasant, pool-lined promenade that runs beside the walls. At the end you'll meet a statue of the 12th century philosopher, medical writer and commentator on Aristotle, Averroës – one of the most famous thinkers of Córdoba's golden age. Near here an arch in the walls readmits you to the Judería.

A sinuous alley (Calle La Luna) leads to a crossroads at which you turn left on Calle Tomás Conde to reach the Plazuela Maimónides. Here the **Museo Municipal de Arte Taurino** (summer: Tues–Sat 10am–2pm and 6–8pm; winter: 4.30–6.30pm in winter; closed Sun pm and Mon) is dedicated to the art of bullfighting. Continue past a statue of Maimónides – a Jewish philosopher whose 12th-century treatises on medicine were translated throughout medieval Europe. To your right you will find the **Zoco**, a handicrafts market whose studios and workshops sell high-quality Córdoban leather goods, jewellery and ceramics.

The Synagogue

Further on, along Calle Judíos, is the **synagogue** (Tues–Sat 10am–2pm and 3.30–5.30pm; Sun 10am–1.30pm) – one of three in Spain that have survived since the golden era. (The other two are in Toledo.) It is remarkable that this small, intimate place of worship still exists: it dates from 1314 and has walls bearing Mudéjar ornamentation and Hebraic

Right: the 12th-century scholar Maimónides

inscriptions. Over the centuries it has served as a hospital for rabies victims, a hermitage, a cobbler's workshop, a school and a warehouse.

After touring the Judería, head back towards the river until you reach Campo Santo de los Mártires square, one side of which is dominated by Córdoba's **Alcázar** (summer: Tues–Sat 10am–2pm, 6–8pm; winter: 4.30–6.30pm; Sun 9.30am–2.30pm). The fortified palace was built by Moorish craftsman for King Alfonso II in the 14th century. The magnificent gardens are probably more interesting than the building itself. When it comes to lunch, the Judería has plenty of good options. Two of the best eateries are **El Churrasco** (Calle Romero 16, tel: 957 290 819) and **Taberna Pepe de la Judería** (Calle Romero 1, tel: 957 200744).

10. CITY WALK AND MUSEUMS *(see map, p43)*

This half-day itinerary takes you to the less-visited eastern sector of Córdoba where the traditional atmosphere of the old city intermingles with the modernism of the new. Venture out in the morning if you like markets and shopping, after lunch if you enjoy the peace of empty streets.

Start in **Calle Cardenal Herrero** and walk east to its junction with Calle Magistral González Francés, at which you can walk up the narrow Calle Encarnación. **Taller Meryan** at No 12 is a workshop that sells a typical range of traditional Córdoban tooled and embossed leather goods. A quintessential part of Córdoba's character, which you will encounter frequently in this walk, is the patio. These inner courtyards were created by the Moors as cool central sanctuaries in which householders could escape the oppressive heat of summer. They often have a central fountain encircled by ferns, and surrounding walls bedecked with brightly flowering pot plants, colourful patterned ceramic plates and cheerful *azulejos*.

Turn right, then left by the Hostal La Milagrosa (on Calle Horno del Cristo) into the **Plaza del Jerónimo Páez**. This square contains the province's **Museo**

Above: taking the weight off their feet in the old Jewish quarter

Arqueólogico (Tues 3–8pm; Wed–Sat 9am–8pm; Sun 9am–3pm), which is housed in a Renaissance palace. Take the pedestrian Calle Julio Romero de Torres, which winds round (past No 19) to descend the Calle del Portillo. At the bottom an ancient archway takes you beyond the old city walls – opposite this is the baroque Convento de San Francisco.

Turn right, cross the road, then take the second left to pass the Hostal Maestre (Calle Romero Barros), which finally delivers you into the charming **Plaza del Potro**. The plaza gets its name from the *potro* (foal) that soars above its gushing 16th-century fountain. A plaque nearby immodestly reminds visitors that Cervantes mentioned the square 'en la mejor novela del mundo' ('in the best novel in the world'). The creator of *Don Quixote* stayed in the plaza's *posada* (inn), which is now an arts centre (free entry). Here you will find a permanent exhibition of *guadamecí* – a style of embossed and coloured leatherwork introduced to Córdoba from North Africa in the 9th century.

Bellas Artes

Opposite is the **Museo Provincial de Bellas Artes** (Tues 3–8pm; Wed–Sat 9am–8pm; Sun 9am–3pm), housed in the former Hospital de la Caridad. It contains an interesting miscellany of Córdoban *objets trouvés* including Roman relics, religious portraits, prints of old Córdoba, one Goya engraving, and some 20th-century sculptures. In the same building, the **Museo Julio Romero de Torres** is devoted to the works of a local painter

(1880–1930) who specialised in erotic portraits of sultry, under-dressed Andalusian women.

At the top of the Plaza del Potro, just after No 15, a small street takes you past a puppeteers' workshop. Here you should turn right round into Calle Armas before heading straight on, via Calle Sanchez Peña, to reach the large rectangular **Plaza de la Corredera**. Traditionally a site for the city's markets, bullfights and entertainment, the galleried brick buildings that enclose the square were built in 1688. Today it is the scene of an easy-going market that is good for clothes, crafts and an assortment of household items.

Further on you will see the restored

Top: the foal that gives Plaza del Potro its name. **Left:** on the Calleja de las Flores **Right:** enjoying the view from the Torre de la Calahorra

columns of a Roman temple standing somewhat bizarrely next to the modern town hall. If you intend to visit the **Palacio de los Marqueses de Viana** (summer: 9am–2pm; winter: 10am–1pm, 4–6pm; Sun 10am–2pm; closed Wed and 1–15 June), turn right here. This is a 16th-century Córdoban stately home that was privately owned until 1980. With no fewer than 13 patios and 38 rooms and galleries crammed with antiques collected from all over the world, it is guaranteed to trigger the imagination. Whirlwind guided tours only.

Continue uphill along Calle Claudio Marcelo, which culminates in Córdoba's bus-clogged central square, the **Plaza de las Tendillas**. For a quieter route, turn left by the Ferreteria Central – which does good handmade calfskin boots – into the pedestrianised shopping precinct of the Calle Conde de Cárdenas. Walking through the precinct you will discover the 16th-century Jesuit church of **Salvador y Santo Domingo**, a monument to St Raphael, and further ahead the curved facade of the 18th-century **Iglesia de Santa Victoria**. Skirting this – to the violin strains that often emanate from the music conservatory in Calle Juan Valera – you reach a main street (Calle Angel de Saavedra) where you turn left to head downhill along Calle Blanco Belmonte towards the Mezquita. There is a good view of its tower from the Plaza Benavente. Take a small alley to the left of this plaza (past No 2) which leads to Calle Velazquez Bosco. This runs down to the Mezquita: on the way take a trip up the **Calleja de las Flores**, the vainest, most photographed street in Córdoba.

Circumvent the Mezquita, head for the Guadalquivir river and cross the Roman bridge to the **Torre de la Calahorra**. This 14th-century tower houses a museum devoted to life in Seville during its Moorish heyday (daily, summer: 10am–6pm; winter: 10am–2pm, 4.30–8.30pm). Exhibits include a model of the mosque as it was before the cathedral was built in its centre.

Medina Zahara

A fitting end to a view of Córdoba in Moorish times is an excursion (by car, taxi or bus) to the ruins of **Medina Zahara**, 8km (5 miles) west of the city. The remains of this once-fabulous palace-city illustrate the rise and fall of the Córdoba caliphate. In 1013, less than a century after Abd Al-Rahman III ordered it built, it was completely razed by rioting Berber soldiers.

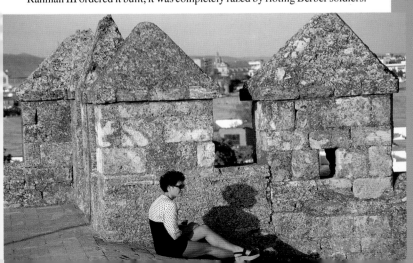

Excursion

11. MONTILLA AND THE SIERRA SUBBÉTICA
(see map, p18–19)

Drive south from Córdoba into the heart of the Montilla region to sample rich Pedro Ximenez wines; cross the mountainous landscape of the Sierra Subbética nature park; return to Córdoba through olive country.

Take the NIV motorway west out of Córdoba, and turn off onto the N331 road, signposted Málaga. This takes you through rolling wheat and sunflower fields, past the castle towns of Fernán Nuñez and Montemayor. After 50km (30 miles) take the turnoff to **Montilla**, the main town in the region.

The principal grape here, the Pedro Ximénez, is said to be named after a German soldier in the Spanish imperial army, Peter Siemens, who brought the original cuttings from the Rhine in the 17th century). It is exceptionally sweet by nature, and its sugar content is further increased by spreading the harvested grapes on mats to roast in the sun. After crushing, fermentation transforms the sugars into alcohol, resulting in wines with a kick of 15–18 percent. Similar to sherry, they range from the crisp, dry and pale fino, to nutty, amber oloroso and amontillado, and velvety Dulce Pedro Ximénez.

Life in Montilla revolves around the wineries, the oldest and most famous of which is Bodegas Alvear, which dates back to 1729. You can visit the cellars of the huge winery complex in the centre of town, where the wine slowly matures in row upon row of ancient oak casks, each holding 500 litres. To visit, tel: 957 664 014.

Head south from Montilla to **Aguilar de la Frontera** and another fine bodega. The small **Toro Albalá winery** (tel. 957 660 046) produces some of the best aged sweet Pedro Ximenez wines in Spain. It also has a curious

museum devoted to old farming artefacts and wine-making paraphernalia.

For ornithologists, a short detour from Aguilar de la Frontera takes you to the lagoon of **Zoñar**, where you can spot various aquatic bird species, including the rare white-headed duck. A marked path around the lagoon starts from the visitors centre on the road between Aguilar and Puerto Alegre.

Back on the main N331 highway, 20km (12 miles) south from Aguilar is **Lucena**, which has a thriving furniture industry. Its large factories and showrooms attract buyers from Córdoba, Sevilla, Granada and the Costa del Sol. Pass this sector to reach the historical centre of Lucena, and one of the region's finest baroque churches, San Mateo.

From Lucena, take the A316 to **Cabra**, the entry point for the Sierra Subbética nature park. The A340 road to Priego de Córdoba takes you through spectacular scenery. For a sweeping view of the region, take a detour to the 1,200-metre (3,940-ft) Ermita de Nuestra Señora de la Sierra shrine.

180-jet Fountain

Priego de Córdoba, 30km (18 miles) from Cabra, is a veritable treasure trove of baroque art and architecture, and its churches, especially La Asunción, San Pedro and La Aurora, are well worth visiting. Also check out the colourful displays of geraniums along the old quarter's narrow streets at the foot of the castle. Finally, before you leave, see the enormous, 180-jet Fuente del Rey (King's Fountain) near the entrance to the leafy Priego park.

Head east from Priego on the A340 to the small town of **Almedinilla**, whose fascinating ruins of a large Roman villa are one of the best preserved of their kind in Spain. The ruins are covered by a protective iron roof. Press on eastwards to reach the N432 highway at **Alcalá la Real**, a town overlooked by La Mota castle. Like other castles in the region, it is evidence of the historical period when these towns guarded the frontier between Christian Spain and the Moorish kingdom of Granada.

Heading north back towards Córdoba, leave the mountains behind and plunge into a boundless landscape of neat rows of olive trees. Some of the finest olive oil in the world is produced in this part of Spain; one of the best-known producers is to be found in **Baena**, 50km (30 miles) from Alcalá la Real. The Nuñez del Prado family has been making *aceite de oliva* for seven generations. You can visit their olive mill, part of which dates from the 18th century, on weekdays; it is situated next to Baena's town park at Calle Cervantes 14.

Leaving Baena and heading north back to Córdoba, pass Espejo and, as a parting shot, yet another picture-perfect castle, this one dating from the 14th century. From here, it is 23km (14 miles) back to Córdoba.

Left: nobody is too young to sample the local wine
Above: an olive farmer poses

Granada

Only 80km (50 miles) from the Mediterranean coast, Granada stands a cool 685 metres (2,250ft) above sea level. Once based around three foothills of the **Sierra Nevada** – Albaicín, Sacromonte and Alhambra – the city now oozes out over the eastern end of the *vega*, the long fertile plain that, in Moorish times, was a vast market garden of orchards, farms and watermills. Further east the snowy peaks of the Sierra Nevada provide the waters for the city's two principal rivers, the Darro and the Genil.

Visitors to the Alhambra are restricted to 7,700 per day. Tickets have three parts: the Alcazaba, the Generalife and the Nasrid Palaces; the latter can only be visited during the half-hour slot shown on the ticket. Tickets can sell out quickly. To avoid disappointment, purchase yours in advance – contact Linea BBV, tel: 902 22 44 60 (from Spain) or 34 913 745 454 (from abroad) or buy direct from BBV banks in Spain. To buy on the day, arrive early. The ticket office is at the bottom of the car park. On Tues, Thur and Sat the Nasrid Palaces also open 10pm–midnight (winter: Sat only 8–10pm).

12. ALHAMBRA: ALCAZABA AND GENERALIFE
(see maps, p55&56)

Spend a day exploring the Alhambra hill, visiting the Alcazaba fortress, the Generalife gardens, Charles V's Palace and the Nasrid Palaces.

To optimise a visit to the Alhambra, you must buy a ticket in advance *(see above)*. Your ticket will show your admission time to the Nasrid Palaces *(see page 57)*: structure the rest of your visit accordingly, saving the Nasrid Palaces for last, if possible.

The traditional approach to the Alhambra involves a steep, half-hour walk up from the Plaza Nueva. After a while the ascent leaves the grimy shops of the Cuesta de Gomérez for the cool woods of the Alhambra hill. Pass through the **Puerta de las Granadas** (Gate of the Pomegranates – the city's emblem) and, taking the left-hand path, you will find yourself outside the citadel's most imposing entrance, the **Torre de la Justicia**. Two symbols above the horseshoe arches of this great Moorish gateway serve as a reminder that you you are entering the world of Islam: a hand represents the faith's five tenets – the oneness of the deity, prayer,

Left: the Alhambra's Patio de los Leones
Right: Puerta de las Granadas

A Brief History of the Alhambra

Construction of the Alhambra began in 1238 under the aegis of Ibn-al-Ahmar, who was the founder of the Nasrid dynasty. Ibn-al-Ahmar rebuilt the ancient fortress of the Alcazaba, originally separated from the main hill by a ravine (now the Plaza de los Aljibes) and diverted the waters of the Darro to supply the new citadel. Most of the palatial splendour you see today was built in the 14th century by Muslim craftsmen who fled here as al-Andalus fell to the forces of the Reconquest.

The Catholic monarchs Ferdinand and Isabella restored parts of the palaces, though the cathedral they installed in the mosque was replaced in the late 16th century by the Iglesia de Santa María. Ferdinand and Isabella also built the Franciscan convent (now the Parador).

Their grandson, Charles V, who demolished more than he replaced, built his palace on the site of the cemetery. With the expulsion of the Moors, several minor earthquakes and a gunpowder explosion in 1590, the Alhambra fell into decline.

Some 200 years later the Alhambra was ransacked by Napoleon's troops. They left it in a parlous state of decay which, ironically, is what endeared the Alhambra to the Romantic writers, artists and travellers then discovering (or inventing) the exotic Spain of the 19th century. 'The Alhambra', Benjamin Disraeli declared in 1830, 'is the most imaginative, the most delicate and fantastic creation that ever sprang up on a Summer night in a fairy tale.' Such eulogistic appreciation of this clapped-out castle goes a long way to explaining why so many tourists gather here today.

By 1870 the Alhambra had been declared a national monument and today it is a UNESCO World Heritage site. You might want to read Washington Irving's *Tales of the Alhambra*, which is on sale everywhere. The writer, an American diplomat, lived here for a few months in 1829.

fasting, alms-giving and pilgrimage; and a key, representing the prophet's power to open and close the gates of heaven.

Alternatively, you can get there by taxi or by bus (every 15 minutes from Plaza Nueva). Either way, it is impossible to miss the massive bulk of **Charles V's Palace** (admission free). Though commissioned in 1526 it was not built until almost a century later. Its stark, haughty, Renaissance grandeur contrasts with the frenzied egg-box ceilings and crazy stuccoing of the Nasrid Palaces. The masterful design by Pedro Machuca is, unfortunately, the architect's only surviving work. Once in its inner courtyard you will appreciate the simplicity and power of Machuca's concept – a circle in a square, executed in unadorned stonework.

Moorish Craftsmanship

To the left of the courtyard is the **Museo de la Alhambra** (Tues–Sat 9am–2.30pm), whose **Jarrón de la Alhambra**, a 14th-century Nasrid vase decorated with gazelles, is worth seeing. The collection has many relics from the Alhambra's glory days: ceramics, *azulejos*, pottery lamps, carved roof-beams, marquetry chess boards, a copper minaret – all of which bring this great Moorish stage set to life. Opposite the museum's exit is the **Museo Bellas Artes** (Tues 2.30–8pm; Wed–Sat 9am–8pm; Sun 9am–2.30pm). Push on through its worthy collection of religious paintings and sculptures and you

Above Right: the Torre del Homenaje (Homage Tower)

will find in the 19th-century galleries a diverting display of Romantic Andalusian art featuring typically coy and picaresque characters.

Continue through the **Puerta del Vino** towards the battlements of the Alcazaba. This is the oldest part of the fortress – some sections date from the 9th century but the two towers overlooking the Plaza de los Aljibes (Square of the Cisterns) date from the 13th century. Their burnt red walls (*al-Hamra* is Arabic for 'the red') remind us that the Alhambra began life as a military garrison. The plaza was once a moat, then an underground cistern.

The Alcazaba's Towers

Enter the **Alcazaba** by the Torre Quebrada (Broken Tower) and wander around the the Torre del Homenaje (Homage Tower) to reach the Plaza de Armas – which in former times was full of houses and barracks. Today only the dungeons and cisterns are visible. On its far side signs guide you towards the main tower, the **Torre de Vela** (Watchtower). En route you might enjoy the little-visited **Jardín de los Adarves** with its terrace offering classic views of the Sierra Nevada. There are yet lovelier views from the top of the Torre de Vela: for centuries the bell in the top of the tower was used to tell the farmers of the *vega* when to irrigate their crops.

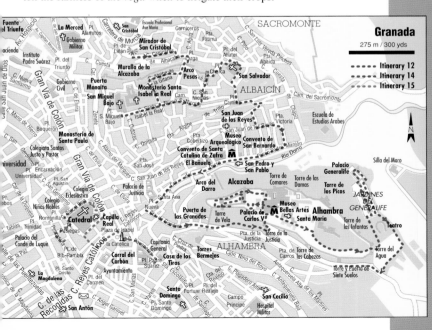

The Alhambra's one-way system directs you down to the battlements and beyond, to the Machuca Gardens. The entrance to the **Nasrid Palaces** follows, but leave that for later. Instead make your way back to Charles V's Palace and around into the centre of the Alhambra precinct. The Calle Real leads past the Iglesia de Santa María to the **Restaurante Polinario**, which offers a fine, inexpensive buffet. Further is the luxury **Parador de San Francisco**, a former convent dating to 1495.

The Generalife

To the right of the Parador is the entrance to the **Generalife**. This was the Nasrid rulers' summer residence, created in the mid-13th century and re-created today as a horticultural paradise inspired by Moorish themes. The lovely gardens incorporate many features similar to those of the palace buildings – hidden entrances, enclosed gardens, pools and trickly fountains. Towards the end of the Generalife the restored pavilions have views over to Sacromonte hill.

To leave the gardens, follow a nearby avenue of oleanders to the estern exit. From here you can walk down beech-lined avenues back into Granada through the verdant Alamedas.

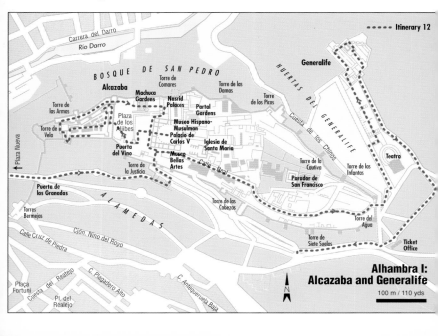

**Alhambra I:
Alcazaba and Generalife**

100 m / 110 yds

The Moor's Chair

A longish walk uphill from the car park, past the cemetery, takes you to the **Silla del Moro**, the 'Moor's Chair'. This is a rock from which, according to the legend, the Moorish king would watch his palace being built. It's well worth the hike just for the view.

Closer to the Alhambra entrance is the **Carmen de los Martires** (Mon–Fri 10am–2pm, 5–7pm), a palace with a large Italian-style garden through which you can stroll. A short distance from here is the **Alhambra Palace** hotel, one of the city's most colourful hostelries. You don't have to be a guest at this neo-Moorish-style fantasy to enjoy a drink in its bar. The bar's terrace has a great view of the city and the *vega* beyond. Crane your neck a bit, and you can also see the snow-capped summit of Sierra Nevada.

The great musician Manuel de Falla enjoyed a similar view from his home nearby. Born in Cádiz, the composer of *Nights in the Gardens of Spain* spent the latter part of his life in Granada, where he was a friend and mentor of the poet Lorca. His former home, the **Casa Manuel de Falla** (tel: 958 229 421), has been converted into a museum that celebrates his life and works. To visit the museum you must call ahead for an appointment.

13. ALHAMBRA: NASRID PALACES AND GARDENS
(see maps, p55&59)

The Nasrid Palaces constitute the inner sanctum of the Alhambra. Beyond the palaces lie some idyllic gardens and patios, in which you might want to while away some leisurely afternoon hours.

The entrance to the Nasrid Palaces is at the far side of Charles V's Palace (Palacio de Carlos V), one of the most outstanding examples of Renaissance architecture in Spain. The first room, the **Mexuar**, was an audience chamber used for judicial and administrative business. In the 18th century it was converted into a chapel. The *azulejos* are from Seville, and in Moorish times there would have been a cupola and lantern rather than the present carved, wooden roof. At the end is the **Oratory**, from which there is the first of many fine views out over the Albaicín and Sacromonte hills.

In Pursuit of the Abstract

Next up is another reception area, the **Golden Room**, which was decorated in Mudéjar style after the Reconquest. Opposite is the **Mexuar Patio** and the facade of the Comares Palace. Here you can observe the intricate patterns of the

Above Left: Generalife Gardens
Right: the Nasrid Palace

plasterwork, constructed in low relief to catch the sunlight. These patterns were used to decorate many of the palaces' walls. Islam proscribes the depiction of the human form and the Alhambra's craftsmen vigorously pursued the abstract: the intention was to direct the eye to the infinite and the mind to the divine by a rhythmic dazzle of repeated floral shapes, interlocking geometric forms, multi-centred grids and ribbons of Koranic inscription joined to proclaim the oneness of God.

Court of the Myrtles

Once you take the short, narrow passage leading into the **Court of the Myrtles** (Patio de Comares) two further principles followed by the Alhambra's architects become apparent: the creation of awe-inspiring effects (often hidden behind bland exteriors and concealed entrances), and the incorporation of natural elements, particularly light and water, as an integral and active part

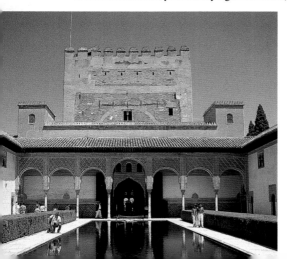

of the architecture. Now you are in the Serallo, the heart of the royal palace where foreign emissaries would have been received.

As you walk alongside the long goldfish pond (in a clockwise direction) you will pass a small niche that allows close inspection of the lovely stalactital stuccowork. The faded colours in its recesses are a reminder that such ornamentation, made from

Above: Nasrid Palace stucco
Left: Court of the Myrtles

a crude assemblage of brick, wood and plaster, was once painted and gilded.

Next you pass through the Barca Gallery, an antechamber to the splendid **Hall of the Ambassadors** where the Moorish kings presided. Take a seat here, the better to contemplate an impressive domed ceiling, a celestial affair of inlaid wood that depicts the seven heavens revolving around the seat

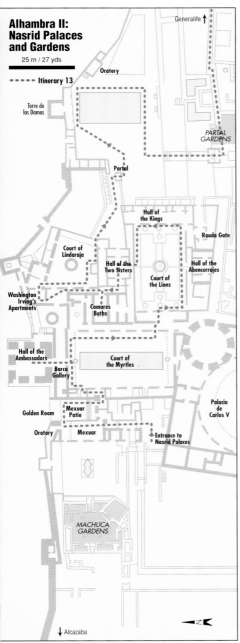

**Alhambra II:
Nasrid Palaces
and Gardens**

25 m / 27 yds

- - - - Itinerary 13

Generalife ↑

Oratory

Torre de
las Damas

PARTAL
GARDENS

Partal

Hall of
the Kings

Rauda Gate

Court of
Lindaraja

Hall of the
Two Sisters

Court of
the Lions

Hall of the
Abencerrajes

Washington
Irving's
Apartments

Comares
Baths

Hall of the
Ambassadors

Barca
Gallery

Court of
the Myrtles

Palacio
de
Carlos V

Golden Room

Mexuar
Patio

Oratory

Mexuar

Entrance to
Nasrid Palaces

MACHUCA
GARDENS

N

↓ Alcazaba

of God. Continue around the Court of the Myrtles and through a short passage that leads into the harem, the private section of the palace and the last to be built. It is heralded by the **Court of the Lions** (Patio de los Leones) which was said to be the decadent swansong of a doomed monarchy. The design represents a symbolic Islamic paradise: an enclosed garden (substitute plants for what is now gravel) with a central fountain from which the four rivers of paradise flow into four restful pavilions surrounded by a forest of marble palms. Around the fountain stand 12 lions, whose significance is not clear: they might represent the signs of the zodiac, or possibly the tribes of Israel.

The sultan and his entourage resided here, and in the adjacent four rooms: to the left as you enter are his wife's apartments (**Hall of the Two Sisters**), which have a cupola said to include more than 5,000 cavities. Opposite this is the **Hall of the Abencerrajes**, which was used for entertainments; notice the beautiful octagonal ceiling. Ahead is the **Hall of**

the Kings, behind which are some alcoves that were once bedchambers. The ceilings above are covered in leather and painted with scenes of courtly life, presumably by a Christian artist commissioned by the Moors.

Royal Baths

Exit the patio through the Hall of the Two Sisters and you will come to the **Baño de Comares** (Royal Baths). The tiled chambers and star-spangled domed roofs constitute the most evocative part of the complex. You can wander down the terraces to the secluded corner of the Alhambra in which the American author Washington Irving lived in 'delicious thraldom' while writing his bestseller. The Lindaraja and Daxara Gardens were both apartments of the harem that were remodelled in the 16th century.

The exit from the palaces near the Torre de las Damas (Ladies Tower) leads to the **Partal Gardens**, which served as the servants' quarters and vegetable plots. Here a kiosk offers the welcome relief of a cool drink. You will pass a pavilion built above the fortress walls that faces a pool guarded by two lion statues which are said to have come from a lunatic asylum that occupied part of the Alhambra during the mid-19th century. Nearby is a small Moorish oratory; further on, ancient towers and modern gardens lead on towards the Generalife.

14. Exploring the Albaicín *(see map, p55)*

Piled up on a steep hill facing the Alhambra, the Albaicín was the heart of Moorish Granada and the seat of the royal court for two centuries before the Nasrids built their palaces on the opposite side of the Darro river. Its pretty streets and houses retain a Moorish flavour.

When the city fell to Ferdinand and Isabella in 1492 the Albaicín had 60,000 inhabitants; by the early years of the 17th century the persecution and expulsion of the rebellious 'moriscos' (Muslims who converted to Christianity) had reduced this figure to 6,000. Traditionally a somewhat impoverished quarter, the Albaicín now constitutes a pleasant, unpretentious maze of narrow streets lined with whitewashed houses, palaces surrounded by high walls, and once-active churches and convents that have fallen into neglect. However, for all the modern-day elements of gentrification that seep through the Albaicín's many alleys and thoroughfares, its Moorish character persists, and the air is delicately perfumed with jasmine and, more prosaically, mule dung. Head for the Albaicín at around midday for lunch and a leisurely stroll: you can climb up from the **Plaza Nueva** but be warned that it is heavy going – it is a lot more advisable to take a taxi or the mini-bus from Plaza Nueva up to the **Mirador de San Cristóbal**.

Top: the fountain in the Court of the Lions
Right: Plaza Larga, the Albaicín

granada itineraries

Walled Gardens

From this Mirador there is an excellent view over Granada and the *vega*: in the foreground you will see the old city walls of the Albaicín. From here you can take Calle Brujones (to the left of a souvenir shop) and turn right to descend a steep cobbled street (Cuesta de San Cristóbal). Soon you will pass two recurring features of the Albaicín: to the left is an *aljibe* (water cistern), to the right a *cármen* (a private walled house with a garden).

Drop down the hill into the Plaza Almona, then turn leftwards to ascend into the **Plaza Larga**. This is the hub of the Albaicín – in the morning it hosts a bustling market, for the rest of the day it is an open-air café and meeting place. In the right-hand corner of the plaza stands the 11th-century **Puerta Nueva**, which has a defensive dog-leg passage. Having passed through the gateway, continue straight through the Placeta de las Minas, then turn right into Calle Aljibe de la Gitana. After a turn to the left you arrive at the small park – the Placeta del Cristo de las Azucenas. This adjoins two of the Albaicín's most famous buildings – the moorish palace of **Dar al-Horra** and the **Monasterio Santa Isabel la Real**, which dates back to 1501.

A Postcard-Perfect View of the Alhambra

Here you are confronted by a choice: you can either turn right towards the palace or continue down the slope and turn right on Calle Isabel la Real, which leads to the monastery. In both cases the route leads to the tranquil **Plaza San Miguel Bajo**, which is a good place at which to stop for a drink or a light lunch. Try Bar Lara, which specialises in meats from the Alpujarras. From the plaza return along the Camino Nuevo de San Nicolás, where a curve to the left will lead you up some steps to the Mirador de San Nicolás and a postcard-perfect view of the Alhambra.

Look straight ahead and you will be able to see the old city walls that run across Sacromonte hill, along with the abandoned caves that once formed Granada's old gypsy quarter. Descend the steps and turn right to reach the small plaza that sits discreetly beside the Iglesia del San Salvador.

From here you can zig-zag your way downhill by any of a number of routes that keep you facing the Alhambra. You should, however, follow the signs to the **Cármen-Restaurante Mirador de Morayma** (Mon–Sat 1.30–3.30pm, 8.30–11.30pm; tel: 958 228 290), which is known as one of the most delightful restaurants in all Granada. This is a place that affords patrons the relatively rare opportunity to enter a flower-filled *cármen*; it also serves local specialities such as *espinacas al Sacromonte* and *habas con jámon*, along with Sierra Nevada cheeses.

Café Society

Probably the easiest route down from here is via Calle Placeta de Toqueros, from which you turn left then right to descend the gentle gradient of the Cuesta de la Victoria. Now you will find youself beside the Darro ravine. The plaza here has a gentle, neighbourhood atmosphere during the day. And it is well worth returning to in the evening when it takes on a relatively cosmopolitan atmosphere and is peopled by café-society dawdlers, basketball players and baked-potato sellers. A range of bars along the **Paseo del Padre Manjón** serve *tapas* and small dishes; La Fuente is the place to hear good-quality Spanish pop music.

From here you can follow the Darro back towards the city centre along a narrow street that is constipated by traffic. On the way you will pass the Casa del Castril, home of the **Museo Arqueológico** (Wed–Sat 9am–8pm; Sun 9am–2.30pm), and **El Bañuelo** (No 31, Tues–Sat 10am–2pm), which houses well-preserved 11th-century Arab public baths with domed roofs and star-shaped vents.

15. THE CATHEDRAL QUARTER *(see map, p55)*

The cathedral, built on the site of a mosque in 1523, is hidden by nondescript buildings below the Gran Vía de Colón. This district of pedestrian shopping streets and leafy plazas is liveliest in the mornings.

Start at the cafés of the **Plaza de Bib-Rambla**, just west of Calle Reyes Católicos. Calle Pescadería leads to the **Mercado Municipal de San Agustin** markets. From the centre of Calle Pescadería take Calle Marqués de Gerona to the Plaza de las Pasiegas. Here you see the main facade of the **cathedral** (Mon–Sat 10.30am–1pm, 4–7pm; Sun 4–7pm), designed in 1667 by Alonso Cano. The cavernous interior, completed in 1714, is austere. The small **museum** (at the opposite end) and the intimate **sacristy** (right as you enter) are probably the most interesting features.

The Capilla Real

On leaving the cathedral turn right into Calle Oficios and the **Capilla Real** (10.30am–1pm, 4–7pm), where you will find the resting place of Ferdinand and Isabella. First you encounter the sacristy (the usual point of entry, via the Lonja, is closed for restora-

Left: the Plaza Isabel la Católica statue

tion), which has a wealth of regal art and treasures. Move on to the chapel, where the marble tombstones of Ferdinand and Isabella are upstaged by the larger ones of Philip the Fair and Joan the Mad, which were placed there by their son, Charles V.

Scholars and Merchants

Back in Calle Oficios you pass the site of Granada's Arab university, **La Madraza**, founded in 1349 by Yussuf I and now part of Granada University. If the door is open you can inspect a small, richly decorated oratory across the patio. Carry on down the street and left through a small arch to enter the Alcaicería, a 19th-century reconstruction of the Arab silk market that originally stood here. Today it is a parade of souvenir stalls. Continue straight on and cross Calle Zacatin, a long pedestrian shopping street, to reach Calle Reyes Católicos. Directly across the road in Calle Lopez Rubio you will see the arch above the entrance to the **Corral del Carbón**, a 14th-century caravanserai that quartered travelling merchants and their pack animals. The interior courtyard, surrounded by three-storeyed galleries, hosts the regional tourist office.

For lunch, go up Calle Reyes Católicos to the **Plaza Isabel la Católica**. The dominant statue commemorates Queen Isabella's support for Columbus. From here you can take Calle Pavaneras to the small, tree-shaded, car-cluttered **Plaza Padre Suarez**, where **Seis Peniques** offers a range of set menus in an alfresco setting opposite the Casa de los Tiros, an early 16th century mansion – note the muskets peeping from the upper windows.

For a classier venue, you may want to try the cellar-restaurant at the bottom of this plaza, **La Alacena** (Tel: 958 221 105).After lunch, return to the **Casa de los Tiros** museum (Mon–Fri 2.30–8pm). Upstairs there is a small exhibition of local 19th- and early 20th-century folk traditions. The best room, the *Cuadra Dorada*, has no displays, but its magnificent Renaissance ceiling is worth a glance in its own right.

Above: the tombs of Ferdinand and Isabel in the Capilla Real

granada itineraries

Excursion

16. SIERRA NEVADA AND THE ALPUJARRAS
(see map, p18–19)

To the Veleta peak in Sierra Nevada; then back down the mountain to explore the Alpujarra region on the southern slopes of the sierra, taking in the villages of Capileira, Bubión, Pampaneira and Trevelez.

Sierra Nevada's Mulhacen is, at 3,500 metres (11,500ft), the highest peak in Iberia. The snow-capped summit of the Sierra, providing a dramatic backdrop to the Alhambra, forms the classic postcard image of Granada. In 2000 Sierra Nevada and the surrounding 214,000 acres were declared a national park. It is also home to Spain's southernmost winter resort: between December and April it has 60km (40 miles) of marked ski slopes at altitudes ranging from 2,100 metres to 3,273 metres (6,900ft-10,750ft).

Much of the mountain is above the tree line, so the scenery is on the stark side when there's no snow, but the combination of high altitude and southern sun supports 4,000 plant species, along with ibex, eagles and an impressive range of butterflies. Hiking, horseriding and paragliding are among the activities on offer in the warmer months.

Europe's Highest Road
In the early years of the 20th century, diehard Granada skiers would lug their skis by mule-back over winding trails to reach the Sierra Nevada slopes.

These days a modern road takes you there in just over half an hour. This, the highest road in Europe, is popular with car manufacturers who want to test new models at high altitudes.

Halfway up the mountain is the El Dornajo Park visitors centre, where you can pick up maps and literature on Sierra Nevada's wildlife and outdoors activities. Further on is the main ski station, Pradollano. This was built with little concern for its aesthetic integration with the landscape, and it remains an ugly mixture of faux-Andalusian buildings, Swiss chalets and faceless concrete blocks. Unless you have business here (such as skiing) it is best to press on to the Veleta, the second-highest peak in the Sierra at 3,470 metres (11,380ft.). The road

Left: Capileira and Bubión

ends within close range of the peak. If it's scenery rather than skiing that you are after, the best time to come is just before or after the ski season, when there is a bit of snow at the top of the mountain.

Pass of the Moor's Sigh

The most spectacular scenery is to be found on the southern slopes of the Sierra, the region known as the Alpujarra. You cannot drive across the top of the mountain to get there (the dirt road is off limits to visitors), so backtrack, towards Granada. Skirt the city, following signs to Motril, on the N323 road. A few miles from Granada is the Suspiro del Moro, (Pass of the Moor's Sigh). The name is a reference to Boabdil, the last Moorish king of Granada, who, heading for exile, paused here for a final, tearful look at the city he had lost to Ferdinand and Isabella. His mother retorted: "Weep like a woman for the city you didn't defend like a man".

Some 37km (23 miles) south of Granada is the turnoff to the town of Lanjarón. Due to several natural springs fed by the Sierra's melting snow, Lanjarón is famous for its mineral-rich water, which is sold all over Spain. And thousands of visitors "take the cure" at the town's *Balneario* (spa).

The town of Órgiva, 9km (5 miles) east of Lanjarón, marks the gateway to the Alpujarra region. Just before the town, take a left fork to the Barranco de Poqueira, the heart of the Alpujarra. Clinging to the valley sides are the villages of Capileira, at the top, Bubión in the middle, and Pampaneira at the bottom. Bubión is the region's tourism centre – here you'll find hotels, restaurants, crafts shops and other indications that the area is no longer "Spain's best-kept travel secret". Capileira is quieter, Pampaneira the most pristine. In Pampaneira you will see the distinctive flat slate roofs of the local architecture, and the postage-stamp farms on terraces carved out of the hillside, alternating with rushing streams and chestnut forests.

Continuing your explorations of the Alpujarra, head eastwards from Pampeneira towards **Trevelez**. The route takes you through increasingly luxuriant, unspoiled scenery, past the small villages of Pitres, Pórtugos and Busquístar. It then climbs towards Trevelez which, at 1,476 metres (4,842ft), is the highest village in the country. Trevelez is famous throughout the country for its serrano hams, which are naturally cured in the crisp mountain air. But don't expect to spot any pigs here. The basic ingredient of serrano hams - pork shoulders and hams - are shipped in from elsewhere to hang in the dozen or so curing cellars at the bottom of the village, where they acquire their distinctive flavour and the privilege of being called Jamón de Trevelez. You can order this ham in any bar in Granada, but somehow it tastes much better up here, on the slopes of Sierra Nevada.

You can return to Granada the way you came or take a longer route, through somewhat bleaker mountain scenery, heading south and east from Trevelez to Torvizcón, then rejoining the original route at Órgiva.

bove: Jamón de Trevelez, a local speciality

Leisure
Activities

SHOPPING

Mass-produced Andalusian mementoes include gypsy costumes, castanets, personalised bullfighting posters, mantillas, Mezquita wine-flasks and Alhambra table-lamps. Beyond these clichés, specialist shops sell quality hats, fans, handmade shawls, guitars and wrought ironwork *(esparto)*.

Leather goods, jewellery and ceramics are widely sold – keep an eye out for good-value shoes, silver filigree, decorative plates and bowls, *azulejos* and kitchenware. Cheap belts, wallets, bags and baskets are sold by African hawkers who will barter.

If you're searching for gifts, consider sherry, convent-made sweets, olive oil, cassettes of guitar music, figs, honey, almonds and saffron. Other favourite Spanish purchases are *cava* (sparkling wine – try the Delapierre or Freixenet labels), cigars from the Canary Islands or Cuba, carved olivewood utensils, terracotta kitchenware, *paella* dishes, candle-holders, *sangría* jugs, Lladró porcelain, *alfombras* (carpets and rugs) and *jarapas* (cotton rugs and car-seat covers).

Seville

Seville's main shopping street is the **Calle Sierpes**. This is the place for fashionable clothes as well as more *típico* fare, from fans to ceramics. Martian (No 48) offers a pleasing display of Sevillian ceramics and pottery. Zadi (No 48) has a serious collection of fans, mantillas and Lladró porcelain, while the old-fashioned Marquedano (No 40) stocks a classic range of Andalusian hats.

To the east, the Plaza de Jesús de la Pasión is the city's matrimony corner, with several jewellery shops. Beyond the northern end of Calle Sierpes you come to the Plaza del Duque de la Victoria, with Spain's largest department store, El Corte Inglés. Around

the corner on Calle Alfonso XII Sevilla Rock sells Spanish pop and guitar music including flamenco and *sevillanas*.

For ceramics, La Alacena (further down Alfonso XII, at No 25) has top-of-the-range china and crockery from La Cartuja factory (now on the Carretera de Mérida). Puerta Triana (corner of Calle Santas Patronas and Calle Reyes Católicos) has a less expensive selection of painted plates, bowls and jugs while across the bridge in Triana, Cerámica Santa Ana (Calle San Jorge 31) is a rambling showroom-cum-pottery with enough antique and modern *azulejos*.

On the east side of the Maestranza bull-ring, Jamón Real I – Esther Fernández Fdez. (Calle López de Arenas 5) sells Extremaduran wines, meats and cheeses, marmalade and home-made wines and liqueurs (it also has a small bar where you can sample products); there's another branch, Jamón Real II, at Calle Pastor y Landero 2.

Being a university town, Seville has many good book shops. One of the best is Vértice, across from the Old Tobacco Factory on Calle San Fernando.

Left: shoe shops abound
Right: the ultimate frilly dress

Córdoba

The English word 'cordwainer' is derived from Córdoba and testifies to the city's long tradition of high quality leather-work. In the area bordering La Mezquita you'll find studios and cobblers' workshops, such as the one at Calle Magistral González Francés 7 which specialises in riding boots.

Silver filigree (*filigrana de plata*) is also common. Look out also for two distinctive types of ceramic plate: the green and white Caliphal pottery based on 10th century Arab designs, and the dark green pottery from Lucena. Montilla wines and anis-flavoured *licor* from Rute are other specialities.

In the small shops and stalls on the Plaza de la Corredera you'll find tyre-soled sandals, iron rings for hanging up flower-pots, barbecue utensils and wickerwork chairs, baskets, hampers and linen chests. Near the Ayuntamiento the *guarnicionería* Rafael Estevez Lopez (Calle San Pablo 6) sells saddles, riding tackle and woollen blankets while the Zoco, the old souk opposite the Synagogue on Calle Judíos 5, is the headquarters for Córdoba Association of Craftsmen, many of whom have their shops here. It is a good place to browse for silver filigree, jewellery, leather work and ceramics.

Granada

Granada's souvenirs play heavily on the city's Moorish past – embossed leather, marquetry chessboards, inlaid furniture, and a distinctive blue and green pottery known as *fajalauza* are the most obvious examples.

The Albaicín is the best place to chance upo these but you'll also find them in the Cues de Gomérez at the foot of Alhambra hil Woven products from the Alpujarras moun tains are worth looking at – the Tejidos Fo tuny workshop (Plaza de Fortuny 1) ha attractive rugs and wall-hangings.

Granada's main shopping area lies sou and east of the cathedral. Calle Pescader has small friendly shops selling meats an cheeses and a stall opposite the Bar Boc has good *fajalauza* pottery. You may fin interesting bargains in the Alcaicería (th old silk-market). For a spot of self-indu gence, buy a box of mouth-watering cake from Flor y Nata (Calle Mesones 51) o Lopez Mezquita (Calle Reyes Católicos 29

Markets

Markets are the best place to buy fresh foo from the countryside: honey, goats' cheese spiced meats, snails, seafood, olives, nut bread and fruit. Produce arkets usually sta early and pack up around 1pm.

In **Seville** every district hosts its own dai fresh produce market – there is one in th Plaza de la Encarnación and another acros the Triana bridge (turn right), on the site o the old Inquisition headquarters. There is small weekday arts-and-crafts market ou side El Corte Inglés in the Plaza del Duqu de la Victoria. In the north of the city there a centuries-old flea market on Thursday i Calle Feria known as 'El Jueves'. Nearb in the Alameda de Hércules a similar bric-a brac market takes place on Sunday morn ings. At the same time there's a bird and pe market (including silkworms) in the Plaza d la Alfalfa, and a stamp-and-coin collector market in the Plaza del Cabildo.

In **Córdoba** the main market venue is th Corredera. In the week a covered *mercad* sells fresh produce while stalls outside sel fabric, clothes, plants and household item On weekends this becomes a flea market.

Granada's nicest market is in the Plaz Larga in the Albaicín, but you'll find a bet ter range in the Mercado de San Agustín o the southwest corner of the cathedral.

Left: ceramics are a popular buy

EATING OUT

In cities like Seville, Córdoba and Granada people never seem to stop eating. Mornings are when work gets done and breakfast is but a meditative moment. Anything goes as long as it's quick: coffee and brandy, chocolate and *churros* (extrusions of sweet battered dough), bread dunked in olive oil, toast and dripping – all taken standing at the bar. By 11am the mood shifts cakewards or to an elevenses ice-cream, but by noon the emphasis changes again as the bar staff start putting out their freshly-made *tapas*.

By 7pm it's time for the *paseo* and an obligatory ice cream, after which the *tapas* appear again around 8pm. Restaurants are in action by 9pm but rarely full before 10pm at weekends they will still be serving new customers at midnight. After dinner, it is time for an oloroso, a sticky cake.

What to Eat

Seville claims to have invented *tapas* (snacks and appetisers) and can even tell you the bar where this national custom originated: El Rinconcillo (near the Santa Catalina church, Calle Gerona 40) where the staff developed the habit of covering a glass of *fino* with a *tapa* (lid) of ham. Today *tapas* are found everywhere and can be anything from a saucer of spiced olives or some slices of *jamón serrano* (mountain ham) to a gourmet dish of oranges, onions and *bacalao* (dried cod), or a hot terracotta dish of *paella*.

A *tapa* or *porción* is simply a taster, while a *ración* is a small dish, often cooked. Lunch is the best time for *raciones* – the daily menu will be written on a board or the dishes just put out on the counter. Often the bill turns out to be as costly as a meal but the taste of *fino* and *gambas* (prawns), or a *cerveza* (beer) and *boquerones* (anchovies in garlic and vinegar), is quintessential Spain. If you're a serious *tapas*-addict head straight for Seville to investigate Modesto (Calle Cano y Cueto 5) or the Hostelería del Laurel (Plaza de los Venerables) in the Barrio Santa Cruz and Casa Manolo (Calle San Jorge) in Triana.

Most bars have an alarming array of mountain hams and spiced sausages suspended from the ceiling, all tagged like prize antiques. You could also try some *salchichón* (salami), *chorizo* (red spicy sausage) or *morcilla* (blood sausage) while *habas con jamón* (broad beans with ham) is a typical Granada dish. *Gazpacho* is another famous Andalusian creation, a chilled soup based on bread and olive oil and flavoured with vegetables and herbs – usually tomatoes, garlic and peppers. The Córdobans make their own, thicker version called *salmorejo* while *ajo blanco* is a white soup from Málaga based on garlic, almonds and fruit.

In restaurants look for regional dishes

Above: courtyard dining

Heavenly Sweets

Sweets, pastries, cakes and biscuits have been made in Andalusia's convents since the Reconquest, a sweet-toothed tradition inherited from the Arabs. Today they can still be bought from the nuns.

The recipe for *yemas* is centuries old, originally made from the surplus egg yolks donated to the convents after the whites had been used to clarify the wines of Jerez and Montilla. Those sold in Seville's San Leandro convent are the most famous *(see page 32)* but every convent makes its own delicacies.

Biscuits flavoured with honey, cinnamon, sesame, ginger or almonds are less sugary – try some *alfajores* or *polvorones* made by the Convento de Santa Isabel de los Angeles in Córdoba (near the Palacio de Viana). For a selection of sweets from Seville's many convent-confectioneries visit El Torno *(see page 27)*.

signposted with words such as *andaluz, a la granadina* or *alpujarreño* (from the Alpujarras mountains). Some chefs embrace Andalusia's Moorish heritage with dishes combining the sweet and the savoury, perhaps by using honey, fruit or raisins to spice meat and poultry. Dishes cooked in sherry or incorporating almonds are common, as are country stews (*cocido* or the simpler *puchero*) which may mix chicken, ham, sausage and egg with *garbanzos* (chick-peas), rice or potatoes.

Despite fields full of vegetables, few seem to make it onto Spanish menus. Asparagus, artichokes, aubergines (*berenjenas*) and peppers do pop up but salad is a more common complement to a main dish. There is nearly always a *revuelto* (scrambled egg dish) on the menu, perhaps mixed with salmon, mushrooms, spinach or asparagusn. *Tortilla sacromonte* is a Granada dish in which an omelette is combined with ham, peas and assorted offal.

Having access to both the Atlantic and Mediterranean coasts Andalusia has plentiful fresh fish and seafood. Tuna has been a staple ingredient since pre-Roman times and sardines, swordfish *(pez espada)* and skate *(raya)* feature on menus. Cuts from

large fish are often served with a saffron paprika or tomato sauce while *zarzuela* is a fish stew with a spiced tomato sauce. Fried fish can be bought in take-away *freidurías*

Desserts always include a choice of fresh fruit or ice cream but in better quality restaurants you'll be able to dither over *tarta de almendras* (almond tart), *crema de membrillo con queso* (quince jelly with cheese), *pastel cordobés* (puff pastry with candied fruit) or the *tocino de cielo* (caramel custard) from Cádiz.

Drinks

Andalusia's most famous drink is sherry, a fortified wine from Jerez de la Frontera. Tthe Spanish will drink it with a meal and indeed whenever they can find an excuse. It is the classic complement to *tapas*.

Fino is the most common drink – a light dry sherry, always served chilled. *Amontillado* is mellower with a nutty flavour and an amber hue. *Oloroso* is mature, dark and rich, often drunk as a dessert wine. *Palo cortado* is richer than *amontillado* but lighter than *oloroso*. You should also try *manzanilla* a *fino* made in Sanlúcar de Barrameda on the Atlantic coast where the salty sea air gives it a distinctive tang.

Andalusian wines are few and come a poor second to their sherries. Exceptions are the excellent strong white Montilla-Moriles produced in Córdoba (*amontillado* means 'like a Montilla'), and the sweet dessert wines made in Málaga from muscatel grapes.

Brandies are also produced around Jerez varying from the cheap, highly addictive Soberano to the luxurious Carlos I. There are also assorted firewaters variously flavoured with almonds, cherries, oranges apricots and anis. Spanish measures of spirits are liberal, so take care.

The predominant beer is made by Cruzcampo – *una caña* is normally taken to mean a small glass of draught, *una cerveza* a large glass or a bottle. *Horchata* is an almond milk while *zumos* are fruit juices freshly-squeezed before your eyes – try a mix of *naranja* (orange) and *limón* (lemon). Bottled water is either *agua con gas* (with bubbles) or *sin gas* (without). If you want to avoid ice ask for your drink *sin hielo*. Black coffee is *café solo*, white *con leche* and *cortado* somewhere in between. Cheers is *salud*!

Where to eat

Specific restaurant recommendations are included in the individual itineraries earlier in this book. Remember that it is quite acceptable to order just a starter or one course if that's all you want. Don't ask for the *menú del día* (menu of the day) when you really mean the *especialidad del día* (speciality of the day) – the first is a basic, low price set-meal, the latter is whatever's fresh and in season. Lastly, keep some cash in reserve as not all restaurants take credit cards.

Price Guide

$$$: more than 30 Euros (5,000 pesetas) for a three course meal with house wine for one.
$$: 15–30 Euros (2,500–5000 pesetas).
$: under 15 Euros (2,500 pesetas).

Seville

Casa Robles
Calle Alvarez Quintero, 58
Tel: 954 563 272
A Seville classic, serving regional specialties in a cosy dining room. The bar is famous for its *tapas*. All major cards. $$

Casablanca
Calle Zaragoza, 50
Tel: 954 224 698
You have to fight your way through the tiny packed bar to get to the small dining room in the back to sample its famous seafood dishes. Closed Sun. Some credit cards. $$$

Corral del Agua
Callejón de Agua, 6
Tel: 954 224 841
In the Barrio Santa Cruz, this elegant restaurant occupies a restored 18th-century house, centred on a pleasant patio with plenty of potted plants and a fountain. Most major cards. Closed Sunday. $$$

Egaña Oriza
Calle San Fernando, 41
Tel: 954 227 211
The modern Basque-Andalusian cuisine in this attractive restaurant next to the Murillo gardens, behind the Alcázar, has earned this long-established venue a reputation as one of the finest eating spots in southern Spain. Closed Sun and Sat lunchtime. All major cards. $$$

Enrique Becerra
Calle Gamazo, 2
Tel: 954 213 049
This small restaurant in an old Seville town house serves traditional Andalusian dishes, and has a very popular *tapas* bar. Closed Sun. All major cards. $$

El Buzo
Calle Antonio Diaz, 5
Tel: 954 210 231
Famous for its much-photographed blue tile façade. Decorated in a marine theme, the speciality here is fresh fish. Some cards accepted. $$

El Cairo
Calle Reyes Católicos 13
Tel: 954 213 089
The dinning room is above the popular tapas bar. Meat dishes are on offer, but the speciality is grilled sea bream or sea bass. Some cards accepted. $$

Right: *tapas* time

Hostería del Laurel
Plaza de los Venerables 5
Tel: 954 220 295
On a small square in the Barrio de Santa Cruz, this picturesque establishment is enormously popular, especially among foreign visitors, for its tapas and is good-value dining. All major cards. $$

La Albahaca
Plaza de Santa Cruz 12
Tel: 954 220 714
One of Seville's prettiest restaurants, in an early 20th century palace in the heart of the Santa Cruz area. The decor and the food are an imaginative mixture of Andalusian, French and Basque influences. Reservations essential. Closed Sun. All major cards. $$$

La Taberna del Alabardero
Calle Zaragoza, 20
Tel: 954 560 637
One of a well-known chain of Spanish restaurants (run by a priest), serving Basque cuisine in a typical Seville setting, with stylish dining areas centred around a cool inner courtyard. All major cards. $$$

Meson Don Raimundo
Calle Argote de Molina 26
Tel: 954 223 355
Near the cathedral, this colourfully-decorated restaurant offers a classic Seville experience. Specialises in meat and game, served in generous portions. All major cards. $$

Ox's
Calle Betis, 61
Tel: 954 279 583
Reputed to serve the best steak in Seville and they have good charcoal-grilled fish too, in a small dining room decorated with understated elegance. Closed Mon and evenings Sun. All major cards. $$$

Taberna La Taurina
Calle Trajano, 44
Tel: 954 380 901
This large, popular bar decorated with bullfight posters serves a good range of tapas and snacks, and they also feature an inexpensive three-course menu at midday. Open noon–4pm and 8pm–midnight, closed Sun. No credit cards. $

Cordoba
Almudaina
Campo Santo de los Mártires, 1
Tel: 957 474 342
Installed in a 15th-century house near the Alcázar, this restaurant serves modern variations of local recipes, using fresh produce. There are various different dining rooms, tastefully decorated, centred on an inner courtyard. Closed Sunday in summer. All major cards. $$$

Bodegas Campos
Los Lineros 32
Tel: 957 497 643
Colourful restaurant in a former wine cellar near the Plaza del Potro, decorated like an upmarket tavern, serving variations on classical Cordoba and Spanish dishes. No dinner Sun. Most major cards. $$$

Casa Pepe de la Judería
Calle Romero 1
Tel: 957 200 744
Situated at the entrance to the Judería, this typical Andalusian town house, decorated with paintings, has a pleasant interior courtyard and a series of rooms where you can enjoy traditional Andalusian fare. All major cards. $$

Left: restaurant in the Barrio de Santa Cruz, Seville

Círculo Taurino
Calle Manuel María de Arjona, 1
Tel: 957 481 862
Bullfighting is the theme, and *rabo de toro* (braised bulls tail) stars on the menu along with other Andalusian classics. Mainly Spanish clientele. Most major cards. $$

El Blasón
Calle José Zorrilla, 11
Tel: 957 480 625
An old inn situated in Córdoba's modern town, and under the same management as the famous El Caballo Rojo *(see below)*. Specialises in a slightly more modern cuisine. All major cards. $$

El Burladero
Calleja de la Hoguera, 5
Tel: 957 472 719
Picturesquely located in the heart of the Judería. Serves traditional Andalusian food, including good game. Most major cards. $$

El Caballo Rojo
Cardenal Herrero, 28
Tel: 957 478 001
Near the Mosque, this esteemed and long-established restaurant is known for unusual Moorish and Sephardic preparations, based on medieval recipes, such as *Cordero a la miel* (lamb in honey). All major cards. $$$

El Churrasco
Calle Romero, 16
Tel: 957 290 819
One of Córdoba's top dining spots. Superb venue (an old house with courtyard in the Judería), excellent service, and wonderful food, incorporating many Andalusian classics. Best to reserve. All major cards. $$

Federación de Peñas
Calle Conde y Luque, 8
Tel: 957 475 427
At the northern fringes of the Judería, this colourful, friendly restaurant is a good budget option for traditional Andalusian fare. Some cards. $

Granada
Chikito
Plaza del Campillo, 9
Tel: 958 223 364
A long-established restaurant (the poet Lorca was a regular), serving good Spanish dishes along with more innovative fare. Best to reserve. Closed Wed. Most major cards. $$$

Cunini
Calle Pescadería, 14
Tel: 958 250 777
This friendly restaurant near the cathedral is the best place for fresh seafood in Granada. Closed Monday. All major cards. $$

Los Manueles
Calle Zaragoza 2
Tel: 958 223 413
Very atmospheric, traditional tiled tavern serving classic Granada dishes such as Tortilla de Sacromonte. All major cards. $

Mirador de Morayma
Pianista García Carrillo, 2
Tel: 958 228 290
Has a fantastic location in a *carmen* (villa with garden) in the Albaicin, with unhindered views of the Alhambra. Regional fare. Closed Sun. Most major cards. $$

Rincón de Lorca
Calle Tablas, 4
Tel: 958 253 211
Located in the Hotel Reina Cristina, this is one of Granada's most reliable restaurants, serving regional dishes prepared with a modern touch. All major cards. $$

Sevilla
Calle Oficios, 12
Tel: 958 221 223
This Granada classic opened in 1930. Close to the cathedral, it is a good place to sample traditional Granada dishes such as *Habas con jamón* (cured ham with broad beans) or *Tortilla Sacromonte* (omelette with lambs brains, ham and vegetables. Closed Mon and Sun evenings. All major cards. $$

NIGHTLIFE

Flamenco

Flamenco's origins are mysterious. Elements of ancient Indian, Arab and Jewish music have been detected in its sorrowful and discordant songs and dances. It was the creation of Andalusia's gypsy communities, particularly those that settled between Seville and Cádiz. As these *gitanos* sought work throughout Spain new local styles developed: by the late 19th century flamenco had shed its peasant image and had its own established rules and repertoire.

Today flamenco is crossing over into jazz and rock, and still evolving. Because it is by nature impulsive and improvised, it does not lend itself to repeated public performance. But every city has its flamenco tourist shows, variously described as *tablaos* or *zambras*. They perform the fast, light-hearted cante chico rather than the slow, knife-in-the-heart *cante jondo*. Most hotels sell tickets, inclusive of transport and a drink.

For something more authentic, try one of the smaller bars or clubs (called *peñas*) where flamenco enthusiasts hang out. Seville is especially well-provided in this respect. Performances are usually impromptu, initiated among a group of clients, usually late at nigh after a certain amount of alcohol . One club that stages top quality flamenco in Seville is La Carbonería *(see page 76)*.

Flamenco Clubs
Seville
El Arenal
Calle Rodo, 7
Tel: 954 216 492
Located in an 18th-century house. Has two shows daily; dinner (optional) is served during the first show.

El Palacio Andaluz
Avenida María Auxiliadora, 18
Tel: 954 534 729
Located in a large theatre. There are tables at the back if you want to enjoy dinner during the show. Opens daily, with two shows.

El Patio Sevillano
Paseo Colón, 11
Tel: 954 214 120
A large tablao, near the river, packed wit tourists most evenings. Two shows a nigh

Los Gallos
Plaza de Santa Cruz, 11
Tel: 954 216 981
By far the best of Seville's tourist *tabla*. Tw shows a night.

Cordoba
Mesón la Bulería
Calle Pedro López, 3
Tel: 957 483 839
Stages flamenco singing and dance. Close in winter.

Tablao El Cardenal
Calle Torrijos, 10
Tel: 957 483 112
Córdoba's best flamenco *tablao* in a 16th century building next to the mosque.

Granada
El Corral del Carbón
Calle Mariana Pineda
In summer flamenco is occasionally stage here, in the courtyard of one of the city' oldest Moorish buildings. Contact the touri office (at the same location) for details.

El Corral del Príncipe
Campo del Príncipe
Tel: 958 228 088
Popular with the Spanish, as well as tourist

Jardines Neptuno
Calle Arabial
Tel: 958 522 533
Granada's most popular venue. Decent pe formances, but aimed primarily at tourists

María la Canastera
Camino del Sacromonte, 89
Tel: 958 121 183
One of the better gypsy *zambras* (cave pe formances) in the Sacromonte Hills.

Reina Mora
Mirador de San Cristobal
Tel: 958 401 265
This long-established club is located at the top of the Albaicin.

Performing Arts

Andalusia has a good range of concerts and theatre performances, and many new venues have opened in recent years. Seville has a year-round programme, although the pace slackens in summer, while Córdoba's Gran Teatro has regular concerts and is the venue for the International Guitar Festival at the beginning of July. The biggest cultural bash, however, is the International Music and Dance Festival in Granada (last week of June and first week of July).

Theatres and Concert Halls
Seville
Auditorio de La Cartuja
Isla de la Cartuja
Tel: 954 216 233
Seating 11,000 spectators, this open-air auditorium has occasional rock concerts and dance performances.

Hospital de los Venerables
Plaza de los Venerables
Tel: 954 562 696
Organ recitals are staged in the chapel of this 17th-century hospice in the Barrio Santa Cruz.

Sala La Imperdible
Plaza San Antonio de Padua, 9
Tel: 954 388 219
Seville's best venue for alternative theatre.

Teatro Alameda
Calle Crédito, 13
Tel: 954 900 164
Stages frequent plays for children.

Teatro Central
Isla de la Cartuja
Tel: 954 460 780
Modern venue featuring theatre, dance and pop jazz and contemporary music.

Teatro de la Maestranza
Paseo Colón
Tel: 954 223 344
Seville's grand, modern opera house stages opera, symphony orchestra concerts, dance, classical and contemporary music.

Teatro Imperial
Calle Sierpes, 25
Tel: 954 226 878
The place to go if you want to see a performance of Zarzuela (Spanish light opera).

Teatro Lope de Vega
Avenida María Luisa
Tel: 954 590 853
Occasional recitals of traditional Spanish singing, but mostly stages plays in Spanish.

Cordoba
Gran Teatro
Avenida Gran Capitán, 3
Tel: 957 480 237
Top venue for music, flamenco and dance

Granada
Auditorio Manuel de Falla
Paseo de los Mártires
Tel: 958 222 188
Home to the Granada Symphony Orchestra.

Teatro de La Alhambra
Calle Molinos, 56
Tel: 958 220 447
Regular plays, concerts and dance.

Above Right: a passionate dance

Bars and Nightclubs

Seville

With its large university population, Seville has countless venues that stay open till the small hours. The best place to check what's on is the monthly *El Giraldillo* magazine, available free from tourist offices or for 150 pesetas at newsstands. The bars in the Barrio Santa Cruz tend to lean towards flamenco. A more contemporary scene exists in Triana, especially on Calle Betis, alongside the river. Another key nightlife zone is the Alameda de Hércules, which has plenty of bars and clubs for gays, straights or both.

Córdoba's nightlife is tamer. In winter the liveliest scene is around the Plaza Tablero or along the Calle Cruz Conde. In summer, action shifts to open air venues along the Avenida El Brillante, on the northern fringes of the city, and in El Arenal, near the river.

In Granada the streets around the University (Calle Pedro Antonio de Alarcón) set the party pace. Bars around the Albaicín, the Plaza Nueva, the Paseo Padre Manjón and the Campo del Príncipe are also populars.

Clubs and discos

Seville

Antique
Matemático Rey Pastor y Castro, Isla de la Cartuja
Tel: 954 462 207
Disco in a former Expo 92 pavilion, with a large dance floor. Appeals to a young crowd.

Catedral
Cuesta del Rosario, 12
el: 954 219 029
Central disco, with regular theme nights.

El Coto
Calle Luis Montoto, 118
Tel: 954 571 072
Exclusive discod.

Fun Club
Alameda de Hércules, 86
Live rock performances are staged most weekends.

La Carbonería
Calle Levies, 20
Tel: 954 214 460
In a former coal yard in the Barrio Santa Cruz, this is a top venue for flamenco, soul, blues, jazz and ethnic music.

Naima
Calle Trajano, 47
Tel: 954 382 485
Animated jazz club, not far from Alameda de Hércules. Regular jam sessions.

Sevilla Salsa
Calle Castilla, 137
Tel: 954 342 204
Latin rhythms in the Triana area.

Weekend
Calle Torneo, 43
Tel: 954 375 012
Live flamenco, jazz and Latin music.

Cordoba

Club Málaga
Calle Malaga
Popular with jazz and blues fans.

Zahira
Calle Conde Robledo
Córdoba's most popular disco.

Granada

Barrio Latino
San Juan de Dios, 12
Salsa, merengue and other Latin rhythms.

Eshavira
Calle Postigo de Cuna, 2
Music bar, focusing on jazz and flamenco.

Granada 10
Calle Cárcel Baja 10
Tel: 958 224 001
Granada's top discotheque.

Sala Cha
Ancha de Gracia, 4
Late-night dance club

SPORTS & ACTIVITIES

Outdoor Activities

Andalusia's sierras lend themselves to a number of outdoor sports and activities.

Hiking, biking and Riding

These sport are especially wellcatered for in the Sierra Subbética in Córdoba, and, in Granada, the Sierra Nevada and the Alpujarras. You can rent bikes in Córdoba (and sign up for a guided bike tour of the area) at Córdoba La Llana en Bici on Calle Lucano 20, next to the mosque. El Mirador riding centre, near the Parador, offers horses for hire, plus organised riding tours of the mountains north of Córdoba.

In Granada, a full range of organised outdoors activities are offered by Ocio Aventura Granada (tel. 958 816 185). For hiking, rock climbing and mountain biking in the Alpujarras contact Nevadensis (Bubión; tel. 958 763 127) and Rustic Blue (Bubión; tel 958 763 381). For organised horse treks in the mountains, try Cabalgar Rutas Alternativas (Bubión; tel. 958 763 136).

In Seville, bikes can be hired from Sevilla Mágica, on Calle Miguel Mañara.

Skiing

During winter, the principal activity in Sierra Nevada is, of course, **skiing**. There's also snowboarding and even dog sleigh rides. For information on winter sports contact the Sierra Nevada ski resort on 958 249 111.

Paragliding

In summer, Sierra Nevada is one of Spain's best venues for **paragliding**. The most active club is Draco (Carretera de Granada Km. 8, Pinos Genil; tel. 958 488 560).

Watersports

Seville is a prime venue for **rowing and kayaking**, hosting the World Championships in 2002. The centre of rowing activity is the Centro de Alto Rendimiento, on Isla de la Cartuja (tel. 954 461 400). The Centro Municipal de Vela sailing club (Puerta Triana, s/n; tel. 954 460 202) organises courses in sailing and windsurfing, aside from staging regular competitions.

Golf

There are four **golf** courses in the Seville area, the oldest being the Real Club Pineda, founded in 1939 (tel. 954 611 400). The best courses are the Real Club de Golf de Sevilla (tel. 954 124 211) and the Club Zaudin, designed by Gary Player (tel. 954 154 159). Serious golfers will find more courses to chose from on the Costa del Sol.

Spectator Sports

Seville has two **football** teams, locked in bitter rivalry: Sevilla, who play at the Estadio Sánchez Pijuán in the east of the city, and Real Betis, headquartered at the Estadio Benito Villamarín in the south. Matches are normally played on Saturday or Sunday – any local paper or Sevillano should be able to tell you when the next fixture is.

Seville also has a top **basketball** team, Caja San Fernando, which play at the Palacio de Deportes de San Pablo on Avenida Kansas City.

Right: water babes

CALENDAR OF EVENTS

The Andalusians joke that every day, somewhere in the region, there's a fiesta going on. When you add in the boisterous stream of cultural events that major cities like Seville, Córdoba and Granada stage through the year it is inevitable that your visit will coincide with a religious holiday, local fair or arts festival.

To find out what's on look out for posters or ask in a hotel or Tourist Office. The following calendar is intended as a rough guide. Always check dates before setting out – in Spain everything is a moveable fiesta.

January

The old year is normally seen off with a cacophony of fireworks and car horns. Tradition says you should swallow a grape (and a sip of *cava* if you're quick) for each strike of the midnight clock. Needless to say **Año Nuevo** (New Year's Day) is a public holiday. **2 January** Granada celebrates the victory of the Catholic Monarchs over the city's Moorish rulers in 1492 with the Día de la Toma (Day of the Capture).
5 January The Cabalgata del los Reyes Magos (Calvacade of the Three Kings) is celebrated with with processions. Next day (6 January) is a public holiday marking Epiphany (Twelfth Night), the day when Spanish children get their Christmas presents.

Above: all the fun of the *feria*

February

1 February Granada holds a fiesta in honour of its patron saint San Cecilio, including a pilgrimage to the Sacromonte catacombs.
28February Andalusia Day, a public holiday

Since the death of Franco, February in Spain has also meant **Carnaval**, an excuse for floats, fireworks, dancing and irreverence

In February or March Seville stages its annual Festival of Ancient Music.

March / April

First week of March Granada stages an International Tango Festival.
Semana Santa (Holy Week). A serious religious celebration, with everything closed on Holy Thursday and Good Friday. Events in Seville are renowned for their dramatic spectacle, but Holy Week is observed with similar panache in Málaga and with equal solemnity in Córdoba and Granada.

Events commence on Palm Sunday when religious and social organisations known as *cofradías* (brotherhoods) carry statues and images from their chapels towards the cathedral. Ornately-decorated floats known as *pasos* transport these figureheads, and behind the *pasos* march *nazarenos*, penitents wearing conical hoods and carrying candles.

In Seville over 100 such processions take place in the course of the week. To witness the most impressive of these tableaux – such as those of El Gran Poder, La Esperanza de Triana and La Macarena which pass through the city in the early hours of Good Friday – consult timetables and official routes published in daily newspapers like *ABC*.
19 March This is San José (St Joseph's Day), a public holiday in some towns.
Mid-April Seville ignites again with its Feria (April Fair), a week-long fiesta of drinking, dancing and bullfighting with horse parades and Andalusian pageantry. Most participants dress for the occasion – *señorita* in bright flamenco costume cling to horsemen in wide-brimmed hats, Sevillian ladies bedecked with flowers and mantillas parade in carriages.

April onwards Seville stages a programme of theatre, dance, exhibitions and music known as 'Cita en Sevilla' (April–June).

May / June

Early May The Día del Trabajo (Labour Day) is a public holiday. Early May is also when the *Cruces de Mayo* (Crosses of May) appear in many towns, elaborately decorated with flowers to herald the arrival of spring. They are best seen in Granada (especially in the Albaicín) or in Córdoba, and form the focus for a fiesta on 3 May.

This first week is also when the sherry capital Jerez de la Frontera holds its annual Horse Fair and Granada holds an International Drama Festival.

Mid May Córdoba comes alive with its charming Festival de los Patios (Patio Festival) usually held in the first fortnight. This is when the Córdobans open up their flower-filled courtyards to all-comers. Concerts and flamenco performances are also held.

End of May Córdoba's festivities culminates in its May Feria, when the streets are graced by elegant horse-riders in Andalusian costume. Every third year the city also stages a national flamenco competition.

30 May Seville honours San Fernando.

Pentecost (Whitsun) at least half a million pilgrims descend on El Rocío, a village north of Las Marismas, the marshland at the mouth of the Guadalquivir river. It is the biggest *romería* (country festival) in Spain.

Corpus Christi (late May or early June) is a public holiday. In Seville and Córdoba choirboys in medieval dress perform set dances before the Cathedral altar, while in Granada the occasion inspires the city's principal fiesta with processions and bullfights, as well as flamenco competitions and a fair.

June / July

Mid-June–mid-July Granada stages its International Festival of Music and Dance which attracts top stars from the world of classical music, jazz and ballet.

Córdoba holds a prestigious International Guitar Festival in the first half of July with classical, flamenco and Latin music. In Seville there is an International Festival of Theatre and Dance.

August

15 August Asunción (Assumption) is marked by a public holiday, and in Seville by the Feast of the Virgen de los Reyes.

Last week The Río Guadalquivir is honoured with a festival in the sherry town of Sanlúcar de Barrameda – events include flamenco competitions and horse-racing along the beach.

September

8 September Córdoba celebrates its patron saint, the Virgen de la Fuensanta.

Last Sunday Fiesta in Granada in honour of the city's patroness, Nuestra Señora las Angustias

29 September in Granada's Albaicín San Miguel is honoured with a procession up to the hermitage San Miguel el Alto.

In even-numbered years Seville stages a Festival of Flamenco at the end of the month.

October

12 October Christopher Columbus's 'discovery' of America is celebrated with a public holiday, Día de la Hispanidad.

24 October Córdoba holds a festival to honour San Rafael.

November

1 November Todos los Santos (All Saints' Day) is a public holiday.

Seville and Granada stage International Jazz Festivals in November.

December

6 December Constitution Day is a public holiday.

8 December Inmaculada Concepción (the Immaculate Conception).

Christmas Navidad is a time for parties, which go on in earnest for the full 12 days.

28 December Spaniards celebrate their equivalent of April Fool's Day, Día de los Inocentes (Day of the Holy Innocents).

Practical
Information

TRAVEL ESSENTIALS

When to Go

Spring is the best time to visit Andalusia: any week from early March, when the orange trees are coming into blossom, to late May, when the fields and roadsides are ablaze with colourful wildflowers. This is also the main fiesta season , when towns and villages decorate their streets with flowers and strings of coloured lights.

Accommodation for Seville's Semana Santa sells out a year in advance despite the fact that the price of a room is around treble what it is for the rest of the year.

For a quieter break try and slip into a week either side of these festivities, or come in autumn – ideally September or October. During the summer the Guadalquivir valley roasts – Ecija, almost mid-way between Seville and Córdoba, is known as *la sartén* (the frying-pan) of Spain – but don't be put off: Andalusian cities, with their narrow streets, patios and gardens are designed for this heat. Granada, with the advantage of being 2,247ft (685 metres) above sea level, is cooler and the Alhambra consequently one of the most delightful places you could spend a Spanish summer.

Climate

In Seville and Córdoba winters are mild (12°C/53°F) with the spring months serving as a delicious bridge into intensely hot summers that soar above 38°C (100°F) in June and July; autumn is a slow cooling-off period as the baked land recovers. In Granada these transitions are more abrupt – spring and autumn are short, summers hot and dry (25°C, 77°F) and winters cold (6°C, 43°F). Rain tends to fall between October and March, often in sudden heavy downpours, but for most of the year the sun shines.

Time Difference

Along with the rest of Europe, Spain is one hour ahead of Britain. Spanish Summer Time runs from the last Sunday in March to the last Sunday in October.

Documents

All visitors require a valid passport or a national identity card (if a citizen of an EU country). Visitors from outside the EU, US, Australia and New Zealand must obtain a visa before entering Spain. Motorists will need an international driving permit (available from international motoring organisations) or EU format three-part driving licence, along with adequate insurance.

Money Matters

The Euro replaces the peseta as Spanish currency in 2002. Euro coins and notes are introduced on 1 January 2002, and pesetas will no longer be used after 1 March. At the time of going to press, 1 Euro (divided into 100 cents) was equal to 166 pesetas..

Health

No vaccinations are required but health insurance is recommended. Form E111 entitles EU nationals to reciprocal medical benefits. A strong sun cream is essential.

Clothing

Seville, Córdoba and Granada are all smart, fashionable cities and their citizens enjoy wearing good clothes. In the summer you'll

Left: for post-cards and letters
Right: a nippy way to get around

need sunglasses, sun-hat and swimming costume, but also something warm for the evenings and air-conditioned buildings; in winter a jumper and anorak will be necessary. Wear comfortable shoes at all times. A money-belt is a good idea.

Electricity

220 Volts. Sockets take round two-point plugs (European size). Most UK appliances will need an adaptor.

Photography

Film is expensive in Spain and some types are not always available. It is best to bring it with you, and develop it when you get home. Carry spare camera batteries.

Customs

There are no restrictions on the import of currencies. You can bring in personal belongings and souvenirs, as well as food for your own consumption. There are no restrictions on quantities of duty-paid goods that can be imported/exported from other EU countries, as long as they are for personal use only.

In July 1999, duty-free sales were abolished between EU countries. Visitors arriving from outside the EU can import (duty-free) 200 cigarettes, 50 cigars or 250g tobacco; 2 litres of wine, or 1 litre of spirits; 500g of coffee beans; 50g of perfume and 0.25 litres of toilet water. Tobacco and alcohol allowances only apply to travellers aged 17 and over.

On Departure

In recent years Spain has had its share of air traffic delays so always confirm your return flight.

GETTING THERE

By Air

Iberia operates scheduled flights from London to Seville, Jerez de la Frontera, Málaga and Granada – some flights involve a stopover at Madrid or Barcelona (Tel: 020-7830

0011 in the UK). Other scheduled carriers operate into Málaga, Jerez de la Frontera and Gibraltar. Charter companies also offer good value flight-only deals to Málaga, Gibraltar and Faro in the Portuguese Algarve – look in the classified section of local and national newspapers.

Seville airport (San Pablo) is 7.5 miles (12km) east of the centre. There is a regular bus connection (30–40 minute trip) into the city or take a taxi for around 2,000 pesetas. For Airport Information tel: 95 444 90 00; Iberia Information, tel: 902 400 500.

Granada airport is served by domestic flights (tel: 958 24 52 00).

Package Deals

Travel companies offer tailor-made holidays visiting Seville, Córdoba and Granada. These include flight, accommodation and car hire. Seville is featured by several city-break specialists.

By Rail

National rail networks offer through-fare deals to Andalusia from the UK; contact Rail Europe, tel: 08705 848848. A high speed rail link has reduced the journey-time between Madrid and Seville to 2 ¾ hours. If you are travelling extensively in Spain it may be worth buying an Inter-Rail card or the Tarjeta Turistica issued by the national rail network, RENFE.

Rail travellers can also tour Andalusia in elegant 1920s style by taking the luxurious Al-Andalus Express, which is known for its gourmet food (bookable in the UK through Mundi Color, tel: 020-7828 6021).

By Road

British coach operators offer services to Spain by road to Seville, details from Eurolines UK(tel: 01582-404511). If you plan to take your own car consider cutting down on the driving by using the French Motorail link between Calais and Nice, contact Rail Europe, (tel: 08705-848848), or sailing from Plymouth to Santander with Brittany Ferries, (tel: 0990-360360).

GETTING AROUND

Seville is ideal for a short break and the best place in Andalusia for street-life, shopping and *tapas* bar-hopping. Córdoba is easily reached from Seville by rail or road and the two cities form a natural pair. Granada and the snow-capped Sierra Nevada are a refreshing contrast to the hot plains of the Guadalquivir valley.

Maps and Guides

The map accompanying this guide contains town plans of all three cities plus a regional map. If you are touring by car and require a larger area than the regional map shows, Michelin map No 446 *Andalusia and the Costa del Sol* is a good choice.

By Car

Drive on the right. Seat belts are compulsory and motoring offences earn on-the-spot fines. In rural areas petrol stations may close on Sundays or for a siesta; most, but not all, take credit cards.

If you take back roads in the countryside you'll have a longer journey but a far more rewarding trip. In the cities you'll just have to take a road that isn't blocked or dug up. The Spanish treat inner-city driving as if it was a motorised bullfight, which means they see it as an art-form and therefore something to be enjoyed.

Car Hire

Compared with most other European countries car hire in Spain is inexpensive. Many airlines and package companies offer good value fly-drive deals, and if you know your requirements it's simplest to book before you arrive.

It's also easy to hire cars in Spain, although some firms will not rent to drivers under 21 or with less than a year's experience. In any case, hire companies will need to see your passport and international driving licence or national driving licence. It is sensible to pay a little extra for Collision Damage Waiver and Personal Accident insurance in addition to the statutory Third Party insurance.

Motorbikes and mopeds offer another way of getting around and are easily rented – the age limits are 18 and 16 respectively.

By Train

There are frequent trains between Seville and Córdoba. Connections from either of these cities to Granada or Málaga (3–5 hours) go via the notorious Bobadilla Junction and normally involve a change of train. The journey up from Málaga to Bobadilla is spectacular.

The Spanish have an alarming number of train classifications. The speediest trains are the sleek *Talgos* (supplements and reservation required), followed by the *Expresos* and *Rápidos* (both quite straightforward trains); then there are the lazy *Directos* and *Interurbanos*, followed by the utterly slothful *Tranvías*. For a timetable ask for an *horario de trenes*.

RENFE Information:
General enquiries Tel: 902 240 202
Seville, tel: 95 454 0202
Córdoba, tel: 957 49 02 02
Granada, tel: 958 27 12 72

By Coach and Bus

Between Seville and Córdoba there's little to choose between train or coach but for the

Right: taking to the open road

longer journey to or from Granada the coach is more direct and arguably more scenic. Always take a coach if you are travelling between Málaga and Granada. One of the most useful companiesis Alsina Graells which operates an express service between Seville and Córdoba as well as other routes from these cities to Granada and Málaga (tel: Seville 95 441 8811; Córdoba 957 23 64 74; Granada 958 18 54 80).

If you are doing a lot of trips in Seville it is worth buying a *bonobus* 10-journey ticket or a *tarjeta turistica* (tourist pass), which is valid for 3 or 7 days. To visit the Itálica ruins take a bus to Santiponce.

In Córdoba the main bus station is situated at Glorieta de las Tres Culturas. In Granada the main station is on the Carretera de Jaén.

By Taxi

Taxis are a cheap and reliable way of getting around these three cities. A green *libre* sign indicates that a taxi is for hire. Agree a price first for long journeys or tours.

Taxi Numbers
Seville Tel: 95 458 00 00/462 22 22.
Córdoba Tel: 957 47 02 91.
Granada Tel: 958 28 06 54.

ACCOMMODATION

Hotels

The best hotels fill up quickly. If you're taking a short break you may prefer to book an all-inclusive flight and accommodation package before you leave, plus car hire if you require it. If you are touring, ring ahead to book a room – the hotel will probably ask you to arrive by a certain time, so ring again to let them know if you expect to be late. Some hotels, such as the Paradors or those close to the Alhambra, are best booked as soon as you know the required dates. Hotels range from 1–5 star.

In the list of accommodation that follows, the approximate prices for a double room with bath are:

$$$ More than 110 Euros (18,000 ptas)
$$ 70–110 Euros (12,000–18,000 ptas)
$ less than 70 Euros (12,000 ptas)

IVA (Spanish VAT) of 7 percent is added to all hotel bills. You may also encounter Hotel Residencias (HR) which only serve breakfast and Apartment Hotels where rooms have kitchen facilities. *Hostales*, graded 1–3 star, are small family-run hotels offering simple accommodation that varies from the brilliant to the dismal – always ask to see the room before you accept.

Other variations are the *Pensión* (P), *Fonda* (F) and *Casas de Huéspedes* (CH). Self-catering apartments (*apartamentos turisticos*) are best booked through an agent. The minimum stay for apartments is normally a week.

A detailed list of accommodation in each of these cities can be obtained in advance of your stay from the Spanish Tourist Office. Paradors (state-run luxury hotels) can be booked in the UK through Keytel International (tel: 020-7402 8182).

Seville

Alfonso XIII
Calle San Fernando, 2
Tel: 954 222 850
Fax: 954 216 033
Old-style elegance prevails in this classic Seville hotel, built in Neo-Mudéjar style in the late 1920s. The public rooms are magnificent, and the bedrooms sumptuous. **$$$**

Casa Imperial
Calle Imperial, 29
Tel: 954 500 300
Fax: 954 500 330
Email: info@casaimperial.com
Homepage: www.casaimperial.com
This stylish hostelry is in a restored 16th-century palace behind the Casa de Pilatos, with four inner patios. 24 suites, each decorated differently, with enormous bathrooms.**$$$**

Doña María
Calle Don Remondo 19
Tel: 954 224 990
Fax: 954 219 546
A great location near the Giralda is a big plus at this old-fashioned hotel. Rooms come in various sizes and styles. There is a rooftop swimming pool. **$$$**

Inglaterra
Plaza Nueva, 7
Tel: 954 224 970
Fax: 954 561 336
Email: hotelinglaterra@svq.servicom.es
Homepage: www.hotelinglaterra.es
Comfortable and friendly, overlooking the Plaza Nueva, a convenient location for touring the city. A British theme prevails in this long-established hotel, which includes Seville's most authentic pub.**$$$**

Los Seises
Calle Segovias, 6
Tel: 954 4229 495
Fax: 954 224 334
Email: seises@jet.es
A unique location in a part of the 16th-century archbishop's Palace, beautifully restored and strikingly decorated to blend old elements with modern design. Rooftop pool with great view of the Giralda. **$$$**

Macarena
Calle San Juan de Ribera, 2
Tel: 954 375 700
Fax: 944 381 803
Email:
melia.confort.macarena@solmelia.com
An elegant, old-style exterior conceals a modern, comfortable hotel, across from the Macarena basilica. With 331 rooms, its a favourite with visiting businessmen. **$$**

Las Casas de la Judería
Callejón de las Dos Hermanas
Tel: 954 415 150
Fax: 954 422 170
Email: juderia@zoom.es
Homepage: http://lascasas.zoom.es
Three old palaces in the Santa Cruz quarter were restored and converted into this maze-like hotel, with a number of inner courtyards, one of the most charming places to stay in Seville. **$$**

Las Casas de los Mercaderes
Calle Alvarez Quintero 9-13
Tel: 954 225 858
Fax: 954 229 884
Email: mercaderes@zoom.es
Homepage: http://lascasas.zoom.es
Centred on a lovely 18th-century patio, this friendly, professionally run hotel located near the Town Hall and close to Seville's main sights is one of the best in its category, combining a charming setting with modern comfort. **$$**

San Gil
Calle Parras, 28
Tel: 954 906 811
Fax: 954 906 939
Around the corner from the Macarena basilica, this hotel offers spacious lodging in rooms with modern furniture and decor, centred on a traditional patio with Seville *azulejo* tiles. There is also rooftop pool. **$$**

Left: vying for visitors' attention

Europa
Calle Jimios, 5
Tel: 954 214 305
Fax: 954 210 016
A pleasant hotel in the budget category, with a cool Andalusian style inner courtyard, offering basic but clean lodgings. $

Puerta de Triana
Calle Reyes Católicos, 5
Tel: 954 215 404
Fax: 954 215 401
Email:
reservashotel@hotelpuertadetriana.com
Homepage: www.hotelpuertadetriana.com
Conveniently located, friendly, efficient and good value, with attractive reception area and pleasant rooms. $

Hostería del Laurel
Plaza de los Venerables, 5
Tel: 954 220 295
Fax: 954 210 450
Email: host-laurel@eintec.es
Homepage: www.sol.com/host-laurel
With one of the best locations in the Barrio de Santa Cruz, this small hotel and restaurant is very popular. The rooms have a basic but clean decor in light-coloured wood. $

Hotel Patio de la Cartuja
Calle Lumbreras, 8
Tel: 4 954 900 200
Fax: 954 902 056
This hotel is housed in a restored 'Corral de Vecinos' (a home shared by several families). The rooms are modern, and some have kitchenettes. Located next to the Alameda de Hércules, with its lively nightlife. $

Simon
Calle García de Vinuesa 19
Tel: 954 226 660
Fax: 954 562 241
Email: simon@jet.es
One of the best-value choices in the centre of Seville, not far from the cathedral, offering no-frills lodgings in an 18th-century house around an Andalusian patio. $

Zaida
Calle San Roque, 26
Tel: 954 211 138
Fax: 954 213 612
Homepage: www.andalunet.com/zaida
This intimate budget hotel occupies a charming 18th-century town house with an attractive Mudejar-style courtyard. $

Cordoba
Conquistador
Calle Magistral González Francés, 17
Tel: 957 481 102
Fax: 957 474 677
This long-established high class hotel boasts an unbeatable location, right next to the mosque. Rooms are large and modern, some have views of the mosque. $$$

Parador de Turismo La Arruzafa
Avenida de la Arruzafa, Córdoba
Tel: 957 275 900
Fax: 957 280 409
Email: cordoba@parador.es
Modern establishment in the parador network which is situated on a hill on the outskirts of the city. Good views. $$$

Al Mihrab
Avenida del Brillante, Km 5
Tel: 957 272 198
This friendly, neo-Moorish style hotel is not far from the Parador, on the foothills north of central Cordoba. Great views. $$

Amistad Córdoba
Plaza de Maimónides, 3, Córdoba
Tel: 957 420 335
Fax: 957 420 365
One of the best options in Córdoba if you want to be close to the sights. Comfortable rooms in two former mansions looking over the Plaza Maimónides. $

Albucasis
Calle Buen Pastor, 11, Córdoba
Tel/Fax: 957 478 625
Family-run establishment offering good value and clean, comfortable lodgings

around a central courtyard in the heart of the old town. **$**

Mezquita
Plaza Santa Catalina 1, Córdoba
Tel: 957 475 585
Fax: 957 476 219
This small hotel in a restored 16th-century palace enjoys a superb location right next to the Córdoba mosque. **$**

Maestre
Calle Romero Barros 4, Córdoba
Tel: 957 472 410
Fax: 957 475 395
Email: hmaestre@teleline.es
Near the historical Plaza del Potro, a small hotel offering good value accommodation in rooms surrounding a cool inner patio. **$**

Granada
Alhambra Palace
Peña Partida, 2, Granada
Tel: 958 221 468
Fax: 958 226 404
Email: reservas@h-alhambrapalace.es
Homepage: www.h-alhambrapalace.es
Situated at the foot of the Alhambra walls, this ochre-coloured neo-Moorish fantasy has good views over the city. The hotel bar and terrace is a popular meeting place for locals and visitors alike. **$$$**

Melia Granada
Calle Angel Ganivet, 7
Tel: 958 227 400
Fax: 958 227 403
Email: melia.granada@solmelia.es
Though not a very romantic option, this is a large, modern and efficient hotel near the post office, in the centre of the city. **$$$**

Parador de Turismo de San Francisco
Alhambra, Granada
Tel: 958 221 440
Fax: 958 222 264
Email: granada@parador.es
Reservations are essential to get into the most sought-after rooms in this hotel belonging to the parador network. The hotel occupies a converted 15th-century Franciscan monastery situated within the Alhambra gardens themselves. **$$$**

Triunfo
Plaza Triunfo, 19, Granada
Tel: 958 207 444
Fax: 958 279 017
Email: h-triunfo-granada@granada.net
Homepage: www.h-triunfo-granada.com
Situated just off Granada's main thoroughfare, the Gran Vía de Colón, the Triunfo is a small but very comfortably appointed hotel. It is also convenient for shopping and sightseeing. **$$$**

Above: Parador de Turismo de San Francisco

America

Real de la Alhambra, 53, Granada
Tel: 958 227 471
Fax: 958 227 470
Email: hamerica@moebius.es
This is a small and intimate family-run hotel with an enviable location within the grounds of the Alhambra. It is closed January and February. **$$**

Alixares

Avenida Alixares del Generalife
Tel: 958 225 575
Fax: 958 224 102
This modern hotel is well located near the Alhambra. **$$**

Palacio de Santa Inés

Cuesta de Santa Inés, 9, Granada
Tel: 958 222 362
Fax: 958 222 465
Email: sinespal@teleline.es
Boasting a great location in Granada's Albaicin quarter, this small hotel occupies a converted 16th-century palace built around a traditional Andalusian courtyard. Rooms are individually furnished with antiques, and some have balconies. **$$**

Reina Cristina

Calle Tablas, 4, Granada
Tel: 958 253 211
Fax: 958 255 728
Email: clientes@hotelreinacristina.com
Homepage: www.hotelreinacristina.com
A friendly and comfortable establishment in an old Granada house, the Reina Cristina is well located midway between the cathedral and the Plaza Bib Rambla. **$$**

Hostal Suecia

Huerta de los Angeles, 8
Tel: 958 227 781
Fax: 958 225 044
Hotel Suecia occupies an old villa at the foot of the Alhambra hill. A pleasant and informal family-run establishment, it offers accommodation in 12 rooms surrounded by a pretty garden. **$**

Pension Doña Lupe

Avenida del Generalife
Tel: 958 221 473
Pension Doña Lupe is a good budget option for those looking for basic facilities but an excellent location right next door to the Alhambra. **$**

Camping

Seville: Camping Sevilla, Carretera N-IV Madrid-Cádiz km534, tel: 95 451 43 79 Located 6.4km (4 miles) from Seville's city centre; open all year round.

Córdoba: Campamento Municipal, Avenida de Brillante 50, Tel: 957 282 21 65. 1.8 km (3 miles) from Córdoba city centre; open all year round.

Granada: Camping Sierra Nevada, Avenida de Madrid 107, tel: 958 15 00 62. Open March–October only.

USEFUL INFORMATION

Tourist Offices

Tourist offices in Spain are generally helpful but always busy – have a list of questions ready. All of them offer free maps and information, and those run by the Junta de Andalusia (listed first below) also have leaflets. Every large city has a Municipal Tourist Office as well (listed second) which primarily dispenses local information. Offices are normally open 9am–7pm Mon–Sat and 10am–2pm Sun.

Seville Av de la Constitución 21, tel: 95 422 14 04; Costurero de la Reina, Paseo de la Delicias, tel: 95 423 44 65.

Córdoba Calle Torrijos 10 (Palacio de Congresos), tel: 957 47 12 35.

Granada Plaza Mariana Pineda 10, tel: 958 22 35 28; Corral del Carbón, tel: 958 22 59 90.

In **London** the Spanish National Tourist Office is situated at 22–23 Manchester Square, London W1M 5AP, tel: 020-7486 8077, fax: 020-7486 8034.

Tipping and Service

Tipping is normal but not obligatory – usually around 10 per cent for taxi-drivers and at least 100 pesetas for hotel staff and waiters. Some restaurants will add a service charge but many people still leave a tip. In bars it will costs more if you sit down at a table and are served by a waiter than if you stand or perchat the bar.

Facilities for the Disabled

Andalusia is a viable destination for disabled travellers, but facilities vary considerably. The best are found in the resorts of the Costa del Sol, although a number of hotels are listed as having facilities for disabled guests. For more information consult a detailed guide such as the Royal Association for Disability and Rehabilitation's annual handbook *Holidays and Travel Abroad* available in libraries or from RADAR, 12 City Forum, 250 City Road, London EC1V 8AF. Tel: 020-7250 3222, fax: 020-7250 0212.

Children

The Spanish think children should be seen, heard and utterly spoilt. They're not just tolerated but enjoyed, and are welcome guests in restaurants. Most hotels can provide cots and highchairs (book ahead) while baby food, nappies, powdered milk and other necessities are available in supermarkets. Babysitters can usually be arranged through hotels, or ask tourist offices about private services available locally. Hire car firms can supply child seats but these should be ordered in advance (take a sun-screen for the windows). It is against the law for children under 12 to travel in the front seat. On RENFE children under four travel free, and under 12 half-price.

Consulates in Seville

Austria
Marqués de Paradas 26
Tel: 95 422 21 62.
United Kingdom
Plaza Nueva 8
Tel: 95 422 88 75.

Right: fun for the young

France
Plaza de Santa Cruz 1
Tel: 95 422 28 96.
Germany
Avda. de la Palmera 19
Tel: 954 230 204.
Netherlands
Placentines 1
Tel: 95 422 87 50.
USA
Paseo de la Delicias 7.
Tel: 95 423 18 85.

MEDIA & COMMUNICATIONS

In Seville newspapers like *El Correo* and *ABC* publish listings of forthcoming cultural events in the city. In addition, a what's on magazine entitled *El Giraldillo* is published weekly and available free from Tourist Offices, museums and cultural venues. In Córdoba the daily paper *Córdoba* has a section of useful information including late-night chemists and train and bus timetables, as does *Ideal* in Granada.

Telephone

Phone boxes take most coins and you need to insert a minimum of 25 pesetas for a local call. Some now take phone cards (*tarjetas telefónicas*) which can be bought from news and tobacco kiosks. Calls can also be made from multi-boothed *cabinas* (kiosks) in the city centre where you pay an assistant after-

wards. These are particularly useful for long-distance calls.

Main Telephone Offices:

Seville: Plaza Nueva 3.

Córdoba: Plaza de las Tendillas.

Granada: Calle Reyes Católicos.

To call other countries, dial the international access code 00, then the country code: Australia (61); France (33); Germany (49); Italy (39); Japan (81); Netherlands (31); UK (44); US and Canada (1). Calls are cheaper between 10pm and 8am.

Phone Access Codes

Direct Enquiries 1003

British Telecom 900 990 044

ATT 900 990 011

MCI 900 990 014

Sprint 900 990 013

INTERNET

Seville, Granada and Córdoba all have cybercafés and Internet bureaus, where you can check up on your email. Rates are around 300-500 ptas. per hour. Only a handful of hotels, in the more expensive categories, have data ports for connecting your laptop.

BUSINESS HOURS

Spanish hours are vulnerable to what happened the night before, but you will find the majority of businesses in action by around 9am. Activity then stops at 1 or 1.30pm –

for the Spanish day is traditionally divided by a long lunch followed by a siesta, a practice well worth observing, especially in summer. Business resumes again about 4.30pm (5pm in summer) and continues until about 7 or 8pm. Government offices often start at 8am and work through until 3pm.

Banks are more punctual, and open 8.30am–2pm Monday to Friday. They are also open for business on Saturdays 8.30am –1pm from October to April. As in the UK, many transactions can also be done at *cajas de ahorros* (savings banks) which sometimes keep longer hours. Money can be changed (*cambio*) at hotels, and bureaux de change travel agents.

Post Offices (*Oficinas de Correos*) open at least 9am–1pm Monday to Saturday, with main ones open all day. Stamps (*sellos*) can be bought in tobacconists (called *estancos*, but look for a brown and yellow 'T' sign saying '*tabacos*'). They can also be bought at most hotel receptions.

Main Post Offices (for Poste Restante (*Lista de Correos*) mail):

Seville: Avenida de la Constitución 32. Tel: 95 421 95 85.

Córdoba: Calle Cruz Conde 21. Tel: 957 478 267.

Granada: Puerta Real 1. Tel: 958 22 11 38.

HEALTH & EMERGENCIES

Beware the sun's beguiling strength. It is very easy to get burnt, even up in the cooler mountains. Use a strong suntan cream and always drink bottled water.

For minor health problems chemists (*farmacias*) are a good source of advice. They are devoted solely to dispensing medication and are marked by a green cross. Don't confuse them with *droguerías* which sell perfume and toiletries. *Farmacias* have a rota of after-hours service (*farmacia de guardia*) – to find this look for a sign posted in the

Left: catching up on the news

window or in the local paper. For a doctor (*médico*) or dentist (*dentista*) ask at a hotel or in the Tourist Office.

State facilities are adequate – form E111, available from the main post offices in the UK, entitles British citizens to certain benefits in Spain, but if you want to take advantage of these you must first get treatment vouchers from the Instituto Nacional de la Seguridad Social (INSS), and then you can only go to doctors who operate the scheme. Medical insurance is a better bet.

Emergencies

Police and Emergency (*urgencia*) 091.
Fire Brigade 080.
Medical emergency: 061
Seville 954 222 222.
Córdoba 957 293 411.
Granada 958 28 20 00.
First Aid station (*Casa de Socorro*):
Seville: Menendez y Pelayo.
Tel: 954 41 17 12.
Córdoba: Avenida Dr Blanco Soler, 4 Tel 957 21 77 78.
Granada: Avenida de la Constitución (Main Hospital). Tel: 958 24 11 00.

Police

Policemen come in three different coloured uniforms. In urban areas the *Policía Nacional* (dark blue uniforms) rule the streets while the *Policía Municipal* (blue uniforms with a white band on their caps) control the traffic. The *Guardia Civil* (olive-green uniforms) rule everything else. Despite the sunglasses and swaggers they're all quite helpful.

Should anything happen tell your hotel or holiday representative, who should then help you inform the Policía Nacional and make a statement for insurance purposes.

Main police stations are:
Seville: Plaza de la Gavidia.
Tel: 954 289 300.
Córdoba: Avenida del Dr Fleming 2.
Tel: 957 47 75 00.
Granada: Plaza de los Campos.
Tel: 958 28 21 50.

Toilets

Pop into a bar, hotel or restaurant and use the *servicios* (sometimes *aseos*) – it is polite to ask permission first.

FURTHER READING

Insight Guide: Southern Spain (Apa Publications, 1999) offers up-to-date information and in-depth essays on Andalusia and the Costa del Sol.

Insight Pocket Guide: Costa del Sol (Apa Publications, 2001). Tailor-made itineraries linking the best of the coast.

Poems of Arab Andalusia translated by Cola Franzen (City Lights Books) will transport you straight back to the world of al-Andalus. Miguel de Cervantes's *Exemplary Novels* are cautionary tales from 17th-century Spain and a good warm-up prior to tackling *Don Quixote* (both Penguin Classics). Washington Irving's *Tales of the Alhambra* is essential Granada reading (you can buy it in Granada as a paperback). *Here in Spain* (Lookout) by David Mitchell is a compendium of quotes from travellers in Spain, including quips from Richard Ford's definitive 1845 guide *A Handbook for Travellers in Spain* (Centaur, 3 volumes) and George Borrow's eccentric bible-hawking autobiography *The Bible in Spain* (Century).

From the 20th century Gerald Brenan's *South from Granada* (Cambridge) describes his life in the Alpujarras in the 1920s; Ian Gibson's *Federico García Lorca* (Faber) is a biography of Spain's greatest modern poet. Alistair Boyd's *The Road to Ronda* (Collins) and Penelope Chetwode's *Two Middle-Aged Ladies in Andalusia* (Century) describe horse-riding trips in the 1960s. Nicholas Luard's *Andalucía* (Century) and Hugh Seymour-Davies' *The Bottlebrush Tree* (Constable) tell of life in an Andalusian village.

In the UK, books on Spain (guides and background reading) can be ordered through world-travel book specialist Daunt Books, 83 Marylebone High St, London W1M 3DE, tel: 020-7224 2295.

The travel guides that replace a tour guide – now better than ever with more listings and a fresh new design

INSIGHT
Pocket Guides

Insight Pocket Guides pioneered a new approach to guidebooks, introducing the concept of the authors as "local hosts" who would provide readers with personal recommendations, just as they would give honest advice to a friend who came to stay. They also included a full-size pull-out map.

Now, to cope with the needs of the 21st century, new editions in this growing series are being given a new look to make them more practical to use, and restaurant and hotel listings have been greatly expanded.

INSIGHT GUIDE

*The world's largest collection
visual travel guides*

*Now in
association
with*

Discovery CHANNEL

ACKNOWLEDGEMENTS

8/9	**Stuart Abraham**
58T, 68	**Junta de Andalucia**
36	**J.D. Dallet**
1, 20, 21, 24T/B, 52, 55, 57, 60, 61, 65, 67, 72, 77, 80, 81, 83, 84, 87, 89, 90	**Jerry Dennis**
11, 13, 32B	**Andrew Eames**
37, 39	**H. Herbeisen/Marco Polo**
64	**Nick Inman**
16, 26, 28, 44T, 46	**Lyle Lawson**
38	**Hidalgo Lopesino/Marco Polo**
10	**José Martin**
34, 35	**Don Murray**
23	**Alice Prier**
27, 29,31, 32T, 33, 40, 43, 44B, 47, 48T/B, 49, 50, 51, 56, 66, 69, 78	**Mark Read**
63	**Capilla Real**
14, 15, 30T/B, 41, 53, 58B, 63B, 71, 75	**Nigel Tisdall**
Cover	**Pictures Colour Library**
Back cover	**Nigel Tisdall**
Cartography	**Maria Donnelly/Apa Publications**

© APA Publications GmbH & Co. Verlag KG Singapore Branch, Singapore

INDEX